HISTORY & GEOGRAPHY 1110
UNITED STATES HISTORY

LIFEPAC Test is located in the center of the booklet. Please remove before starting the unit.

Author:
Alpha Omega Staff

Editor:
Alan Christopherson, M.S.

Media Credits:
Page 21, 72: © Photos.com, Thinkstock; **37:** © joeygil, iStock, Thinkstock; **39:** © Bronwyn8, iStock, Thinkstock; **41:** © GeorgiosArt, iStock, Thinkstock; **44:** © Ingram Publishing, Thinkstock; **45:** © SmileLikeUMeanIt, iStock, Thinkstock; **60:** © Brand X Pictures, Stockbyte, Thinkstock; **61:** © Russell Barnett, Thinkstock; **63:** © tntemerson, iStock, Thinkstock; **70:** © National Archives and Records Administration; **77:** © ER09, iStock, Thinkstock; **79:** © DeepInsights, iStock, Thinkstock; © Thinkstock, Stockbyte, Thinkstock; **84:** U.S. Air Force Staff Sgt. Jette Carr; **89:** © Kirill Sinani, Hemera, Thinkstock.

804 N. 2nd Ave. E.
Rock Rapids, IA 51246-1759

United States History

Introduction

The history of the United States is a fascinating subject. Its roots go back to the Middle Ages when people first began to realize that life might extend beyond their immediate villages. In time, they ventured out and found prosperous cities and unusual items that would make their lives easier and more interesting.

American colonists were no different. They, too, desired the freedom to live and to worship without restrictions. Eventually, they came to a new land and established a government that would permit these freedoms and self-determination. The new country grew, attracted people from other lands and became prosperous. When outside forces threatened this country, the citizens came to its defense.

In this LIFEPAC® you will study and review the facts about the founding of the United States, the industrial and technological changes that occurred during the 1800s, the wars that were fought, the depression that was survived, and the programs of the presidents.

Objectives

Read these objectives. The objectives tell you what you will be able to do when you have successfully completed this LIFEPAC. When you have finished this LIFEPAC, you should be able to:

1. Explain the changes in Europe that led to the exploration of America.

2. List the events in Europe that inspired the colonization of America.

3. List restrictions placed on the colonies by Britain.

4. Explain the causes and results of the French and Indian War.

5. Explain the causes and results of the Revolutionary War.

6. List major battles of the Revolutionary War.

7. Explain the formation of the Constitution and the colonial government.

8. Explain the administrations of Presidents Jefferson, Monroe, Jackson, and Lincoln.

9. List the causes and the results of the War of 1812, the Civil War, and the Spanish-American War.

10. Explain the causes of slavery.

11. Describe the Reconstruction period in the South.

12. Explain the effect of the Industrial Revolution on lifestyles in the United States.

13. List the causes and the results of World War I.

14. Explain the causes and the results of the Great Depression.

15. List the provisions of Roosevelt's New Deal.

16. Identify the causes and the results of World War II.

17. Identify the causes and the results of wars in Korea and Vietnam.

18. List the major contributions of the administrations of Presidents Kennedy, Johnson, Nixon, and Ford.

19. Explain the reasons for President Nixon's resignation.

20. List the major contributions of the administrations of Presidents Carter, Reagan, George H. W. Bush, Clinton, George W. Bush, Obama, and Trump.

21. Explain the major events shortly before and after the New Millennium.

22. Explain international events that have occurred in recent years.

Survey the LIFEPAC. Ask yourself some questions about this study and write your questions here.

_____

_____

_____

_____

_____

_____

_____

_____

_____

_____

_____

_____

_____

_____

_____

_____

_____

_____

_____

_____

1. FOUNDATIONS OF DEMOCRACY

In this section, you will briefly review life in medieval times in order to better understand American history. You will trace the changes that occurred because of the Crusades and because of the adventurers who were sparked by curiosity to see what lay outside their own villages. You will review the colonization of America and the reasons that motivated people to leave their homes in Europe and travel to the New World.

Section Objectives

Review these objectives. When you have completed this section, you should be able to:

1. Explain the changes in Europe that led to the exploration of America.
2. List the events in Europe that inspired the colonization of America.

Vocabulary

Study these words to enhance your learning success in this section.

astrolabe	An instrument used to observe the sun, moon, and stars.
advocate	To favor or support.
capital	Money or property.
colonize	To found or settle a territory.
diagnose	To recognize or identify by examination.
erect	To construct.
haven	A safe place.
infest	To overrun or inhabit.
ingenuity	Cleverness; originality.
inhabitant	Permanent resident.
maneuver	To make a series of changes in direction.
mercantilism	An economic theory that increased the power and wealth of nations.
perish	To be destroyed or to die.
persecute	To harass, annoy, or oppress those who differ in origin or beliefs.
unearth	To discover or disclose.

Note: *All vocabulary words in this LIFEPAC appear in* **boldface** *print the first time they are used. If you are not sure of the meaning when you are reading, study the definitions given.*

MEDIEVAL SOCIETY

Life during the Middle Ages was uncomplicated but difficult in terms of personal freedoms. People were members of one of three classes: noblemen, serfs, and clergy. They and other members of their particular family remained rigidly locked in the same class. Most houses were small cottages with dirt floors and simple furniture that was fashioned of available materials, such as straw and wood. Food primarily consisted of bread and vegetables with little meat and no herbs or spices to prevent spoilage or to enhance flavor. Opportunities to alter the course of one's life were available to only those few born into wealth. Even they had limited options in education and travel.

The noblemen owned all the land and the houses as well. The serfs worked the land for the noblemen and had few, if any, freedoms. Serfs could not own land, find another job in another place, nor even leave the village without the nobleman's permission. The villages in which the people lived provided for their needs. A mill for grinding grain, a blacksmith shop, and a tannery for making leather goods were typical of most villages. Only a few products were brought into the village from outside. Mistrust and petty jealousies constantly arose among the landlords, or noblemen, who frequently feuded and fought for power.

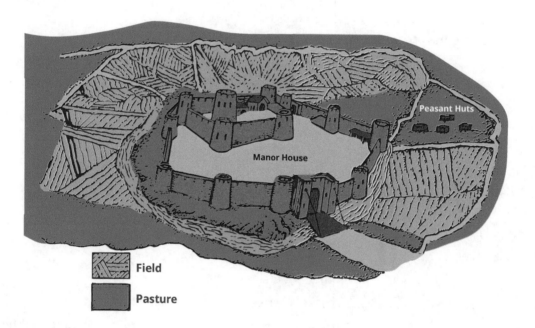

Peasant Huts

Manor House

Field

Pasture

The clergy was not involved in these jealousies about lifestyles; they attended to preaching, teaching, and caring for the sick. The clergy upheld the doctrines of the Catholic Church and gave stability to the society. A new development was about to occur, however, that would change the lives of all the people of this age. These remarkable changes came out of the quest of the Christians to recapture the Holy Land—they called themselves Crusaders.

In 1095 the Pope urged the Christian people of Europe to attempt to recover the Holy Land from Muslims. The Muslims were intent upon forcing people everywhere to accept the teachings of the Islamic religion. Although the Crusaders were successful in recapturing the Holy Land, they were unable to hold it. The struggle to regain it continued

for the next two hundred years. In this endeavor the Crusades failed; but they did revive trade, which lead to the growth and development of cities.

The Crusades also caused the people of Europe to come into contact with a more advanced culture. For example, they learned that other people had spices to season food and sugar to sweeten it. They discovered beautiful gems, fabrics, and perfumes. They found new drugs with which to heal the sick. They also learned about luxuries for their homes and new foods to make life easier and more interesting.

To obtain these items, trade between the East and West began. The usual exchange for goods, gold and silver, was not plentiful in Europe; therefore, such goods as wine, furs, and grain were traded in exchange for the desired goods from the East.

As trade increased, merchants became more prosperous and began to move into the cities and the towns. With the increase in the size of towns and cities, the need arose for peace and order to be maintained through a form of government.

The new middle class merchants, made wealthy by trade, now questioned the authority of the landholders. The freed serfs also moved to large cities to work or to become involved in trade. Medieval life and the feudal system it had fostered began to break down.

Match these items.

1.1 _____ mercantilism

1.2 _____ astrolabe

1.3 _____ maneuver

1.4 _____ capital

1.5 _____ unearth

a. to discover or disclose

b. to make a series of changes in direction

c. an economic theory that increased the power and wealth of nations

d. an instrument used to observe the sun, moon, and stars

e. money or property

Complete these answers.

1.6 People in the Middle Ages were members of these three classes:

_____

_____

_____

1.7 During the Middle Ages land was owned by _____ .

1.8 Medieval society suffered from constant conflict because of

_____ .

1.9 The group that was unconcerned about different lifestyles because their duty was to care for the

souls of the people was the _____ .

1.10 In 1095, a pope persuaded the people to recapture the Holy Land from the _____ .

1.11 What were the causes of the breakdown of medieval society?

_____

_____

_____

_____

_____

_____

_____

NEW IDEAS

New thinking and new ideas were important also in changing people's lives. In addition to the trading of goods, the Crusades were responsible for the trading of ideas among people. The explorations of Marco Polo, for example, were significant because they unearthed new products for trade and new ideas for the people to ponder. Marco Polo also returned with tales of ports at which hundreds of boats were docked waiting to be loaded with silk, fine woods, gold, and precious stones. Marco Polo spoke of cities with beautiful buildings, apartments, and houses with places for travelers to rest comfortably.

The people of Western Europe had little education and most had never been outside their own villages; therefore, they were fascinated by Marco Polo's stories. They, too, wanted to be able to read, to write, and to travel. This thirst for knowledge signaled the beginning of the Renaissance period in Europe.

The Renaissance opened new worlds for the people. Young men began to study art and literature and to learn to write in their own language instead of in Latin. Science also made progress during the Renaissance. People invented instruments such as the **astrolabe** and the compass to help sailors **maneuver** their ships with greater accuracy. Maps and charts were also improved to enable sailors to maintain a more accurate course in every voyage across the sea.

As people became more interested in reading and writing, a way to quickly reproduce printed material was needed. The solution came when Johann Gutenberg invented a printing press with movable type in the mid 1400s. Gutenberg's invention did more to spread the words of learned people than anything else of the times. As ideas were spread by the printed word, the effects of the Renaissance were firmly established throughout Europe and Asia.

Complete these answers.

1.12   The significance of Marco Polo's trip to the Far East was that he returned with stories of

_____ .

1.13   What three events led to the Renaissance?

_____

_____

_____

1.14   The immediate result of the Renaissance was the expansion of _____ .

1.15   The results of the invention of the _____ was the quick production of writings.

POLITICAL STRUCTURE

With the accumulation of **capital** and the policy of **mercantilism** came a new political structure of national states or countries. The kings built these states with the support of the townspeople who were wealthy and could finance the kings. The kings, in turn, hired soldiers to fight for the townspeople and to insure peace in the villages. Spain, Portugal, France, and England had kings who brought separate states together into one nation.

Increased trade brought in more capital. With sturdy vessels and improved methods of navigation, merchants were able to ship goods safely by way of the Atlantic Ocean. Trade centers flourished and the increased capital allowed countries to finance voyages of discovery.

Mercantilism became the economic policy of the new nations. Wealth was measured by the amount of gold and silver in each country's treasury.

Each nation tried to be the leader in sales of goods abroad and each one set up trading posts and colonies in many parts of the world. These trading centers helped the nation gather enough raw materials and food to assure self-sufficiency. The colonies needed finished goods from the mother country and traded raw materials for those goods. That process of trading assured the mother country of surplus gold and silver in the treasury.

The theory of mercantilism meant that the government encouraged trade, commerce, and explorations. Such explorations led to the establishment of new colonies in Africa, India, and the Far East. Governments eventually supported the colonization of the New World.

Complete these statements.

1.16 Trading centers in other countries helped the mother country gather sufficient

_____ and _____ for her own use.

1.17 The economic policy of the new nations was the theory of _____ .

1.18 In addition to voyages for trade, countries financed voyages of _____ to find new lands.

1.19 Kings supported the concept of national states because the townspeople could

_____ the king.

1.20 Exploration led to the establishment of new colonies in _____ ,

_____ , and _____ .

EARLY COLONIZATION

In the 1500s, when most European countries were **colonizing** in other lands, England was not motivated to venture beyond its shores. England was slow to colonize because of political struggles between crown, clergy, and nobility. The results of this struggle, however, would eventually strengthen England's future colonies in their development of self-government. The threat of Spain also kept the English close to their shores. Spain was determined to re-establish the Catholic Church in England although the English were satisfied with the Church of England. England was successful in keeping the Spanish away, but they continued to fear future attacks and the possibility of a takeover by Spain.

Changes in England's thinking about colonization occurred at the urging of Richard Hakluyt, an English geographer. Hakluyt convinced England that without colonies it could never match the powers of Spain and Portugal. He argued that establishing colonies in the New World would insure England the raw materials it needed and would provide a better life for Englishmen. Hakluyt's persuasion was the motivation for England's future colonization of Virginia, the New England colonies, the Middle Atlantic colonies, and the Southern colonies.

The first colony in Virginia was on Roanoke Island. The mystery surrounding the disappearance of that colony has fascinated historians through the ages. Although Sir Walter Raleigh organized the voyage to Roanoke, he never visited the settlement. The real mystery was determining what happened to the original **inhabitants**. When English supply ships returned to the island in 1591, the island was deserted and no trace of the settlers was ever found.

The first permanent English colony in the New World was at Jamestown, Virginia. That expedition began on December 20, 1606 and consisted of 105 men, including craftsmen, farmers, doctors, and adventurers. The men searched for a particular location for their settlement that would give them a view of the sea and of approaching ships and that would provide them protection from the Native Americans. A peninsula on the James River proved to be an ideal location for the Jamestown settlement.

Once the ideal site for a settlement was found, the settlers became more interested in exploring the land and searching for gold and silver than they were in building houses and planting crops. Rats also **infested** the grain supply and destroyed much of it. Because of their lack of preparation for survival, more than half the settlers died from disease or from the result of Native American attacks in the first few months after their arrival at Jamestown.

Without John Smith's guidance at the settlement, the entire population might have **perished**. Smith took charge and ordered the planting of crops and the **erection** of buildings. Under Smith's direction some colonists fished for food; others went to live with friendly Native American groups. Smith's method of dealing with the Native American people enabled the colony to survive. The survival of Jamestown has been solely attributed to John Smith's **ingenuity** and his leadership. Smith, however, did have enemies. Dissatisfaction with Smith came to a head when Smith returned from a trip to visit Native American tribes without the gold and silver he had been sent to find. Smith's enemies were angry, **diagnosed** him as too ill to remain in Jamestown and sent him back to England to receive proper medical care.

Without Smith's leadership, the settlers once again encountered problems. New settlers arrived at Jamestown and their arrival even further strained the low food supply. That winter, over four hundred people died, and those who survived did so by eating roots and snakes.

Just as everyone had given up hope for survival, Lord Delaware arrived with three ships filled with supplies and a new charter that established representative government in Virginia. The charter set up an assembly consisting of a governor, a governor's council, and elected representatives from each settlement in Virginia.

Shortly after the establishment of representative government in Virginia, in 1619, the first ship of women arrived in Virginia. Homes and families could then be started in the colony. Enslaved people from Africa also arrived soon. Some colonists came as indentured servants and agreed to work in the colonies in return for their passage to Virginia.

Match these items with their definitions.

1.21	_____	advocate	**a.**	a safe place
1.22	_____	colonize	**b.**	to overrun or inhabit
1.23	_____	diagnose	**c.**	cleverness; originality
1.24	_____	erect	**d.**	to harass, annoy, or oppress those who differ in origin or beliefs
1.25	_____	haven	**e.**	to favor or support
1.26	_____	infest	**f.**	to be destroyed or to die
1.27	_____	ingenuity	**g.**	to recognize or identify by examination
1.28	_____	inhabitant	**h.**	to construct
1.29	_____	perish	**i.**	to found or settle a territory
1.30	_____	persecute	**j.**	permanent resident

Answer these questions.

1.31 Why was England late to establish colonies in other parts of the world?

_____

1.32 Who was the person who caused England to become interested in colonization?

_____

1.33 What was the first attempted colony in Virginia?

_____

1.34 What happened to that first colony in Virginia?

_____

1.35 What were two reasons why the Jamestown colony was situated where it was?

_____

_____

1.36 Who was the person most directly responsible for the survival of the Jamestown colony?

_____

1.37 What three bodies were part of Virginia's representative government?

_____

_____

_____

COLONIZATION OF NEW ENGLAND

The New England colonies were Plymouth, Massachusetts Bay, Rhode Island, Connecticut, and New Hampshire. Unlike Virginia, settled primarily as a colony to provide raw materials to England, the New England colonies were settled by people who had experienced religious **persecution** in England.

The religious motivation for colonization in America began with Martin Luther and the Reformation many years before the New England colonies were established. During the Reformation, the religious world divided either to follow Martin Luther or to remain with the Roman Catholic Church. Henry VIII, king of England, opposed Martin Luther's Protestant teachings and was loyal to Catholic beliefs. However, in order to divorce his wife, Catherine, Henry declared himself the head of the English Catholic Church and broke ties with the Pope. That action established the Church of England.

Under the reign of Elizabeth I, the Church of England, now Protestant, became the official church under law. Many people, called Puritans, were not happy with the church because of its ceremony, frills, and its teachings. They wanted to purify the church by removing all traces of Catholicism.

The Puritans wanted the Church of England to become more Calvinistic in its theology and practices. Some Puritans believed that the only way for them to solve their problems with the Church of England was for them to separate from that church. These Separatists were considered by Elizabeth I to be dangerous and rebellious. Laws were passed to contain the Separatists and to break up their meetings. The persecution continued even after Elizabeth's death when James I became king. Some Separatists traveled to Holland where they received a measure of religious freedom, but they were not happy with the lifestyle or customs there and many decided to emigrate to the New World.

Plymouth. Plymouth was settled by Separatists who were later called Pilgrims. To gather money to travel to the New World, the Pilgrims sold their goods and bought shares in a joint-stock company. The London Company guaranteed the Pilgrims religious freedom in return for settling on company land in Virginia.

They set sail on the Mayflower in the fall of 1620 and landed on the tip of Cape Cod two months later. They knew this land was outside the boundaries of Virginia, but they decided to stay there for the winter. While they were on board, the Pilgrims elected John Carver as their governor. They also wrote an agreement called the Mayflower Compact that provided for majority rule on any laws established by the group.

Massachusetts Bay. Massachusetts Bay was settled by a group of wealthy Puritans who were given permission to settle in New England under the name of the Massachusetts Bay Colony. Their experiences with religious persecution in England were similar to those of the Separatists. The Puritans had several advantages over the Separatists. They found a loophole in their charter and took the charter with them to assure freedom from England's supervision.

The government in the Massachusetts Bay Colony was not democratic. At first, only a few settlers were permitted to vote. Later, all adult, male church members were allowed to vote. Even when an assembly was established, the elected representatives were closely controlled by the governor. Judges administered the laws of the colony and the church. Little distinction was made between a civil crime and a religious crime.

The colony was controlled by Puritan ministers who set behavior standards for everyone in the colony including non-Puritans. They also set up a system of education for young people so that they could learn to read the Bible and they established Harvard College to prepare young men for the ministry. Those settlers who disagreed with the Puritan leaders were banished from the colony. The Puritans, who had come to the New World to achieve religious freedom, denied similar freedom to those who disagreed with Puritanism.

Massachusetts received a new charter in 1691 and became a royal colony. Although it retained its basic government, its governor was now appointed by the king. All males who owned property were allowed to vote. Religious freedom was assured to all Protestants. With the new provisions of the charter, the Puritan clergy was less powerful. The colony, however, remained large, prosperous, and powerful in New England.

Rhode Island. Roger Williams, an **advocate** of religious freedom and pastor of the church of Salem, was banished from the Massachusetts colony because he spoke out against the Puritan church. He believed that Native Americans should be paid for lands settled by the colonists. He also believed that government affairs and church affairs should be separate.

Consequently, he purchased from the Native Americans the land that is now Rhode Island and founded the Providence Plantations in 1636. In 1644, Williams obtained a charter from the king that provided for an elected governor and an assembly. Williams decreed that no religious laws would be made and that government would not interfere in religion. Williams's commitment to religious freedom attracted many new immigrants, including Jews and Quakers, who had been discriminated against in England.

Connecticut. The desire for a freer system of government than the one in Massachusetts inspired Thomas Hooker to found a settlement in Connecticut. In 1636, his congregation in Newton left on foot for the Connecticut River valley where they settled at Hartford. Later other settlers founded Wethersfield and Windsor. The three communities formed the self-governing colony of Connecticut and drew up the Fundamental Orders of Connecticut. This document served as a model of constitutional thinking from which future state constitutions would develop.

New Hampshire. Located north of Massachusetts, New Hampshire became a **haven** for early settlers who were uncomfortable with life in Massachusetts Bay. Eventually, New Hampshire received its own charter in 1679 and became a separate colony.

Place these events in their proper order.

1.38 _____ Fundamental Orders of Connecticut

_____ Massachusetts becomes a royal colony

_____ Providence Plantations is founded

_____ Puritans travel to Holland

_____ Pilgrims set sail on the Mayflower

_____ the Protestant Reformation

_____ Puritans settle Massachusetts

Complete the following.

1.39 The chief motivation for the settling of New England was _____ .

1.40 The influence of the Reformer, _____ was evident in Puritan theology.

1.41 The Puritans who sought refuge in Holland were called _____ .

1.42 The agreement the Pilgrims wrote while they were aboard ship on their way to the New World was the _____ .

1.43 Identify two reasons Roger Williams was banished from Massachusetts:

_____

_____

_____

_____

1.44 The model document from which future constitutions would develop was the

_____ .

COLONIZATION OF THE MIDDLE AND THE SOUTHERN COLONIES

The growth of America progressed rapidly with the settlement of both the Middle and the Southern colonies. The Middle colonies were Maryland, New Jersey, Pennsylvania, Delaware, and New York. The Southern colonies were Virginia, Georgia, North Carolina, and South Carolina.

The Middle Colonies. Maryland was the first proprietary colony. The charter was given to George Calvert, Lord Baltimore, who had complete control of the colony. Maryland was founded as a refuge for Catholic Englishmen. When Calvert died, his son, the second Lord Baltimore, inherited the grant. Although the charter of Maryland said that men were to have the vote on all laws, Calvert refused to let the assembly do more than approve laws. The colonists showed their resentment until Lord Baltimore finally permitted the Maryland assembly to propose and approve laws.

By 1649, most settlers in Maryland were Protestants. To preserve the freedom of Catholics to worship, the assembly passed the Toleration Act, which guaranteed religious freedom to those who professed faith in Jesus Christ. It was not, however, as broad a guarantee of religious freedom as that in Rhode Island.

New York, or New Netherlands as it was previously called, had been a Dutch colony until 1664. New York had an interesting history. As a Dutch trading post, its population grew slowly. The patroon system was the reason for slow growth. The patroon was similar to the landowner of medieval times and the people he brought to New Netherlands were treated like serfs. As a result, very few people settled in New Netherlands, but the patroons became wealthy and powerful families that are still prominent today.

New Netherlands angered the English because it was a center of illegal trade. American colonists could avoid English regulations and taxes by shipping goods through New Netherlands. King Charles of England offered New Netherlands to his brother James, the Duke of York, if James could conquer it. The people of New Netherlands were not willing to fight because they could see little difference between Dutch rule and English rule. James was able to conquer the colony without a fight. He then named it for himself.

Pennsylvania was founded by William Penn as a haven for the Society of Friends, or Quakers. It eventually became one of the most successful proprietary colonies. In addition to the Quakers, Germans and Scotch-Irish also settled in Pennsylvania. Soon, Philadelphia became the largest and busiest city in the colonies and was called "the gateway to the American West."

The government of Pennsylvania was democratic and had an elected council that advised the governor and an assembly that passed laws. William Penn is credited with having had the most democratic political system in the world at that time. Complete religious freedom was possible for all the people in the colony.

Penn also treated the Native American people fairly. Colonists paid for the land that they settled and the merchandise sold or traded to the Native Americans by the colonists had to be of high quality. As a result of Penn's fair treatment of the Native Americans, they rarely attacked, and both the Native Americans and the colonists lived in peace and prosperity.

New Jersey was settled by a group of wealthy Quakers who purchased the western part of the state from its owner. The Quakers were not fully accepted in England. They vocalized against war and the government. Many were imprisoned and all were excluded from government, the military services, and the universities. These exclusions convinced the Quakers that they must leave the country, and some found relief from oppression in New Jersey.

Delaware was purchased from the Duke of York by William Penn because Penn's first grant of land had no coastline. The land became a part of Pennsylvania, but it was later made into a separate colony, named Delaware.

The Southern Colonies. Georgia was founded as a buffer to keep the Spanish from moving further north and to serve as a refuge for English prisoners. James Oglethorpe founded the colony in 1732. He was to control the colony for twenty-one years, after which it would become a royal colony.

Oglethorpe and his associates hoped the settlers would produce silk and wine for the mother country. Although Oglethorpe advertised widely for settlers, few people seemed interested; and the colony eventually became settled by land-hungry people. Later the king took control and slaves were imported to work on cotton and rice plantations.

The Carolinas were originally settled as one colony. King Charles II permitted a group of eight men to found a colony between Virginia and Spanish Florida. They expected to make large amounts of money from the sale of land, but their ventures were unsuccessful and little occurred in the colony.

Soon, differences between the northern and the southern parts of the colony were evident. Some of the people in the southern part owned large plantations, but most of the people in the north, such as the Quakers and the Germans, grew tobacco and corn and raised livestock on small farms.

The Quakers and the Germans worked the land themselves, but some of the southern inhabitants employed slaves and indentured servants to do the work. Eventually, the colonists petitioned the king to become separate colonies and in 1729 the separation occurred.

Match the motivation for the settling of each colony.

1.45	_____	New York	**a.** haven for Quakers, one proprietor
1.46	_____	Maryland	**b.** lands sales to get rich
1.47	_____	Delaware	**c.** refuge for Quakers; group of wealthy owners
1.48	_____	Pennsylvania	**d.** Dutch trading post
1.49	_____	Georgia	**e.** provided a coastline for Pennsylvania
1.50	_____	Carolinas	**f.** refuge for English Catholics
1.51	_____	New Jersey	**g.** a buffer against northern expansion of Spanish colonies

Match the colony with its founder.

1.52	_____	Maryland	**a.** William Penn
1.53	_____	New York	**b.** George Calvert
1.54	_____	Pennsylvania	**c.** James Oglethorpe
1.55	_____	New Jersey	**d.** James, Duke of York
1.56	_____	Georgia	**e.** William Penn
1.57	_____	Delaware	**f.** wealthy Quakers

✓ **CHECK** _____ _____
  Teacher   Date

↺ **Review the material in this section in preparation for the Self Test.** The Self Test will check your mastery of this particular section. The items missed on this Self Test will indicate specific areas where restudy is needed for mastery.

SELF TEST 1

Answer *true* **or** *false* (each answer, 1 point).

1.01 _____ Democracy flourished in medieval society.

1.02 _____ The Crusades created a demand for goods among the people.

1.03 _____ The Crusades were successful in that the Holy Land was recaptured and retained.

1.04 _____ Italian merchants expanded their trade market because of the Crusades.

1.05 _____ The Renaissance was the beginning of learning for Western Europeans.

1.06 _____ After the Renaissance, trade was greatly restricted.

1.07 _____ England began colonizing in the late 1400s and early 1500s.

1.08 _____ The first attempted colony in Virginia was Roanoke Island.

1.09 _____ Many of the American colonies were settled by groups of people who sought religious freedom.

Complete the following (each answer, 3 points).

1.010 People in the Middle Ages were members of one of these three classes:

_____

_____

_____

1.011 Two reasons the breakdown in medieval society occurred were:

_____

_____

1.012 The Crusades were an attempt to recapture the Holy Land from the _____ .

1.013 An invention of the Renaissance that helped sailors to accurately maneuver their ships was

_____ .

1.014 After the Renaissance, _____ became the economic policy of new nations.

1.015 For some time, the English had little interest in colonizing because _____

_____ and _____ .

1.016 The very earliest religious motivation that led to colonization in America was the

_____ led by Martin Luther.

1.017 The _____ and the _____ began colonies in America to avoid persecution in England because of their religion.

1.018 The Jamestown colony in Virginia was settled to provide _____ for England.

1.019 The Maryland assembly passed the _____ to preserve rights of Catholics to worship.

Match the following (each answer, 2 points).

1.020	_____ Marco Polo	**a.** founder of Rhode Island colony
1.021	_____ Johann Gutenburg	**b.** persuaded England to colonize
1.022	_____ Richard Hakluyt	**c.** founded Maryland colony
1.023	_____ Sir Walter Raleigh	**d.** invented the printing press
1.024	_____ John Smith	**e.** founded Pennsylvania
1.025	_____ Roger Williams	**f.** returned with tales of riches and modern buildings in eastern cities
1.026	_____ George Calvert	**g.** leader of Jamestown settlement
1.027	_____ William Penn	**h.** founder of Roanoke colony
1.028	_____ James Oglethorpe	**i.** took over New Netherlands from Dutch settlers
1.029	_____ James, the Duke of York	**j.** founded Georgia colony

59 / 74

SCORE _____

 **CHECK** _____ _____

Teacher   Date

2. BEGINNINGS OF UNITED STATES DEMOCRACY/ REVOLUTIONARY WAR

The colonists had originally been enthusiastic about the accession of George III. Soon, however, they became disillusioned and even rebellious. The colonists were unhappy with the trade restrictions and taxes placed on them. Still harder to accept by the colonists were the British restrictions placed on their personal rights and liberties. The trade restrictions and taxes were evidence enough to the colonists that they were not free. Although the French and Indian War was a victory for the colonists, the upheaval in the colonies over the lack of freedom was probably a more important motivation for the eventual revolution.

In this section you will review the events that led to the Revolutionary War. You will also review the early developments in colonial government including the Constitution of the United States and the organization of the federal government.

Section Objectives

Review these objectives. When you have completed this section, you should be able to:

3. List restrictions placed on the colonies by Britain.

4. Explain the causes and results of the French and Indian War.

5. Explain the causes and results of the Revolutionary War.

6. List major battles of the Revolutionary War.

7. Explain the formation of the Constitution and the colonial government.

Vocabulary

Study these words to enhance your learning success in this section.

annex . . . . To add on or attach.

balk . . . . To stop or refuse to do something.

barter . . . . To trade.

draft . . . . To make a preliminary plan.

furor . . . . Fury or rage.

immune . . . . Protected from or unaffected by something.

precipitate . . . . To bring on or hasten.

revoke . . . . To withdraw or repeal.

self-determination . . . . Freedom to decide something by one's own free will.

RELATIONS WITH BRITAIN

After the colonies were established, Britain neither bothered them nor placed restrictions on them at first. As time passed, however, Britain's posture with the colonies was more and more restrictive. In time, restrictions became excessive.

Trade. Britain's history of mercantilism and its desire to be a world power motivated it to pass laws that placed restrictions on colonial trade. One such series of laws was called the Navigation Acts of 1660. The first Navigation Act required that all ships carrying goods between Britain and America be British-built or owned. Articles such as tobacco, sugar, indigo, and naval stores, could be sold only to Britain by the colonists. In addition to the Navigation Acts, the British passed the Writs of Assistance. The Writs of Assistance gave officials the right to enter private homes and to confiscate anything that the owner was unable to prove was not smuggled. These laws, however, were not strictly enforced because Britain hoped to keep the colonists friendly in case of a war between Britain and France. After 1763, Britain began to enforce the Navigation Acts.

Other acts that the British imposed and that the colonists thought were unfair were the Wool Act of 1699, the Hat Act of 1732, the Molasses Act of 1733, and the Sugar Act of 1764. Each act was a ban of a product from export to another colony or to Europe. The British also restricted manufacturing in the colonies. The Hat Act was designed to restrict the manufacture and the sale of beaver hats. The Iron Act of 1759 similarly prohibited the building of iron mills and steel furnaces. Raw iron, however, could be shipped to Britain duty free. Another way the British attempted to hold back economic growth was by controlling currency. The colonists were forced, in many cases, to **barter**, or to trade raw materials for the goods they needed, because currency was not available.

French and Indian War. The French and Indian War settled the question of which country controlled the North American continent. Both Britain and France were powerful, proud countries and each country wanted to dominate the colonies. The extreme differences in the customs and the lifestyles of these countries created friction between them.

The French colonies spread over a large area in North America from the Mississippi River valley, along the Great Lakes to eastern Canada and through the land to the Allegheny and Appalachian mountain ranges. The British colonies, which spread along most of the eastern coast, had a much larger population than the French colonies. Nevertheless, the climate was ripe for war between the two countries.

The British and the French had fought a series of wars in Europe that lasted about seventy-five years, but none had much effect upon the colonies until the French and Indian War. That war began when frontiersmen were encouraged to settle the Ohio valley. The governor of New France was angered by this move and decided to build forts along Lake Erie to the Ohio River to keep the intruders out.

In retaliation, Lieutenant Governor Dinwiddie of Virginia decided to build a fort where the Ohio River met the Allegheny and the Monongahela rivers. George Washington and 150 other men were sent to build the fort, but Washington decided to go against the French instead. Washington and his men defeated the French and then began to build the fort called Fort Necessity. Soon the French advanced on Fort Necessity and defeated Washington's men. This battle was the first battle of the French and Indian War.

The British decided to strengthen their forces by uniting the colonies and called a meeting in Albany, New York. Seven of the thirteen colonies sent representatives to the meeting. Benjamin Franklin proposed the formation of a legislature that would consist of a president general appointed by the king and a council whose members would be chosen by colonial legislatures. The legislature would deal with Native American affairs. This plan, called the Albany Plan, was refused by both the colonies and the British. The British preferred to deal with the colonies individually instead of as a group.

The British sent to the New World an army under the leadership of General Edward Braddock. That army was defeated by the French and their Native American allies in the Ohio valley.

In another battle in New York, Colonel William Johnson secured the aid of the Iroquois people and ended French control of New York by defeating the French at Lake George. Later, General James Wolfe captured several New York forts by sailing up the St. Lawrence River and attacking the city of Quebec. Montreal, Detroit, and other French forts along the Great Lakes were eventually captured by the British and these defeats ended French rule in North America. The treaty that officially ended the French and Indian War is known as the Treaty of Paris of 1763.

The French and Indian War resulted in Britain's becoming the leading colonial power in the world. To the colonial settlers, the defeat of the French meant that the colonists no longer needed to fear intrusion by the French. It also brought a feeling of independence to the colonists because they had gained valuable military experience and felt confident they could defend themselves.

Match the following vocabulary words with their definitions.

2.1 _____ barter

2.2 _____ revoke

2.3 _____ annex

2.4 _____ furor

a. to add on or attach

b. to trade

c. fury or rage

d. to withdraw or repeal

Complete the following statements.

2.5 Three acts that were designed to restrict the manufacture of products in the colonies were

the _____ , the _____ , and

the _____ .

2.6 The war that settled the question of which European country controlled the North American

continent was the _____ .

2.7 Before the war most British colonies were spread along the _____ .

2.8 The colonists gained _____ and _____
experience as a result of the French and Indian War.

REVOLUTIONARY WAR

The Revolutionary War was preceded by a number of restrictions that many colonists found intolerable. For example, the Navigation Acts were more strictly enforced than they had been prior to the French and Indian War. The war had also been expensive and the British believed the colonists should help pay for it. King George also believed the colonists were becoming too independent and he wanted to bring them under stricter controls.

Restrictions. The British, therefore, passed a series of restrictions on colonial freedoms. One of these was the Proclamation Act of 1763. Its purpose was to restrict the colonists to the Atlantic coast by closing to them all newly acquired lands west of the Allegheny Mountains. Another restriction was the Grenville program designed to raise more money in the colonies. The Chancellor of the Exchequer, Lord Grenville, ordered an increase in old taxes as well as some new ones on many imported goods. With this program came the Quartering Act, which required that British troops be stationed in the colonies and actually fed and housed by the colonists. The colonists detested this act as an intrusion of privacy.

The Stamp Act of 1765 was another restriction that angered the colonists. It placed a tax on all newspapers, pamphlets, legal papers, calendars, and even playing cards used by the colonists. In retaliation, the colonists set fires, rioted, and debated against the act. Patrick Henry was perhaps most vocal against the act and warned the king of the consequences of the act. Henry's statements were so harsh that many people called them treason. The House of Burgesses in Virginia, however, taking the initiative, wrote the Virginia Resolves condemning the Stamp Act and saying that only the colonial government had the right to levy taxes.

The Stamp Act caused such **furor** among the colonists that a secret organization called Sons of Liberty was formed. Its members were some of the leading citizens in the colonies, including Paul Revere of Massachusetts. Members of the organization drove out stamp-tax collectors and forced merchants not to pay the tax. The group also enforced an unofficial boycott of British goods.

In 1765, representatives from nine colonies met to write a protest of the Stamp Act. The representatives wrote a "Declaration of Rights and Grievances" that stated their loyalty to the British but their opposition to the tax. They insisted that the colonists had the right to tax themselves. Because of this opposition and because exports from Britain to America were declining as a result of the boycott, the Stamp Tax was finally repealed.

Although the Stamp Tax was repealed, the British proposed a series of taxes on other goods. The colonists again protested and boycotted British goods. Many colonists were accused of violating British laws and were sent to Britain for trial. As the boycott of British goods continued to be successful, Britain sent more troops to Boston to maintain order. The severe loss of business to Britain prompted by the boycott forced the British Parliament to repeal all taxes except the one on tea. The colonists were not worried, however, because they could smuggle tea that was cheaper than British tea. Problems were brewing in Boston where British troops were stationed. A riot broke out and British troops fired shots into a crowd killing five people. This incident increased the hatred the colonists felt for the British.

Tempers continued to flare and the British continued to lose money on unsold tea. In an effort to solve the problem, King George agreed to sell tea at a lower price than smuggled tea. Colonists opposed this move because they feared the colonial tea business would suffer. The British, however, sent ships loaded with tea to the colonies. Colonial officials in Philadelphia and New York refused the tea, but the governor of Massachusetts allowed the tea-laden ships to dock. The colonists were so angered that they dressed as Native Americans, went aboard the ship and threw the tea into the harbor. This was the so-called Boston Tea Party.

As punishment for destroying the tea, the colonists were subjected to a series of acts called the "Intolerable Acts." Under these acts the port of Boston was closed and the charter of Massachusetts was **revoked**. Town meetings were not permitted without the consent of the governor and all officials were appointed by the governor. More British troops were sent in and were stationed at the colonists homes. The Northwest Territory, which was partly owned by Massachusetts, was **annexed** by Quebec. The severity of the Intolerable Acts further united the colonists against the British.

First Continental Congress. To overcome the problems with Britain, the colonists called the First Continental Congress in September, 1774. Fifty-six delegates from twelve colonies met in Philadelphia. Among those present were Samuel Adams, John Adams, Patrick Henry, Richard Henry Lee, and Joseph Galloway. The representatives eventually wrote a Declaration of Rights and Grievances, which denounced the Intolerable Acts as unjust and unconstitutional.

The representatives also prepared a list of colonial rights that included life, liberty, property, and the right to control taxation in the colonies. The representatives agreed that no goods should be bought from Britain until the Intolerable Acts were repealed. The colonists were also urged to arm themselves. The colonists anticipated that the Declaration of Rights and Grievances could lead to war. Before it recessed, the First Continental Congress agreed to meet again if the grievances against Britain were not settled.

| The Boston Tea Party

Match the following.

2.9	_____	Grenville Program	a. boycott of goods by British colonists
2.10	_____	Proclamation Act of 1763	b. British troops in the colonies were housed and fed by colonists
2.11	_____	Stamp Act of 1765	c. increase in old taxes and new taxes on imported goods to raise money for Britain
2.12	_____	Declaration of Rights and Grievances	d. closed the port of Boston
2.13	_____	tax on tea	e. closed all newly acquired lands west of the Allegheny Mountains to colonists
2.14	_____	Intolerable Acts	f. only tax on goods that remained after colonist boycott
2.15	_____	Quartering Act	g. tax on newspapers, pamphlets, legal paper, calendars, playing cards

Place a check beside each correct answer.

2.16   The First Continental Congress was called on

_____   December 25, 1775.

_____   June 1789.

_____   July 1776.

_____   September 1774.

2.17   The Declaration of Rights and Grievances drawn up by the First Continental Congress denounced

_____   the Stamp Act.

_____   the king.

_____   the Intolerable Acts.

_____   the Parliament.

2.18   Before it recessed, the First Continental Congress agreed to

_____   write a Declaration of Independence.

_____   take up arms against Britain.

_____   meet again if grievances against Britain were not settled.

_____   elect George Washington President.

2.19   The representatives drew up a list of colonial rights, which included

_____   life, liberty, property, and taxation control.

_____   liberty, fraternity, and happiness.

_____   liberty and due process.

_____   the right to boycott.

2.20 The representatives anticipated that the Declaration of Rights and Grievances could lead to

_____ a compromise.

_____ more taxes.

_____ war.

_____ another boycott.

2.21 Which one of these men was not a representative to the First Continental Congress?

_____ John Adams

_____ Lafayette

_____ Patrick Henry

_____ Joseph Galloway

SECOND CONTINENTAL CONGRESS

In an effort to determine the colonial position toward Britain, the representatives of the Second Continental Congress drew up a "Declaration of the Causes and Necessity of Taking up Arms," which explained to the king and to Parliament the reasons the colonists were fighting the British in Boston. The explanation was called the Olive Branch Petition. The British refused to discuss the petition and prohibited all trade with the colonies. The king also sent 30,000 troops and foreign mercenaries called Hessians to stop the fighting.

Members of the Second Continental Congress decided to establish an army and to choose George Washington as its commander-in-chief. Two battles in Boston encouraged the colonial army. The army was able to hold the British two out of three times when the British Army tried to ascend the hills into Boston. In the other battle the Patriots dragged a cannon into Boston and placed it on a hill overlooking Boston Harbor. The British retreated to Nova Scotia as the Patriots entered Boston and held it.

While the battle continued in Boston, Ethan Allan seized Fort Ticonderoga in New York and the British lost the battle at Crown Point. Fighting also occurred in the Carolinas. The Patriots defeated a group of colonists who had taken the side of the British, and a British attack on Charleston was unsuccessful.

Even with Patriot success on the battlefield, many colonists wished for reconciliation with Britain. As the British continued to send more troops and to employ more foreign mercenaries, the colonists became more angry and began to talk of independence from Britain. Thomas Paine's booklet "Common Sense" was just such an argument for independence. Paine argued convincingly for independence and "Common Sense" became widely read. Paine's writing is believed to have influenced popular thought to the extent that the colonists began to demand independence.

As the Second Continental Congress continued to meet, the representatives became more vocal about independence from Britain. In June, 1776, Richard Henry Lee of Virginia said that his colony had directed him to present a resolution which stated, "That these United Colonies are, and of right ought to be, free and independent States, that they are absolved from all allegiance to the British Crown, and that all political connection between them and the State of Great Britain is, and ought to be, totally dissolved." A committee was appointed to **draft** a declaration of independence and Thomas Jefferson was delegated to write the document. The Congress adopted the Declaration of Independence on July 4, 1776.

The Declaration of Independence expressed a bold new idea about the rights of people. Before this time people believed that the only rights they had were those granted them by their government. The Declaration of Independence also broke all ties with Britain. The colonies became **self-determining**.

The Declaration of Independence is often described as the turning point in colonial relationships with Britain. People were forced to determine whether they sided with Britain or with the colonies. The Declaration of Independence was, in a sense, a declaration of war. The Continental Army was untrained and lacked equipment, while the British Army was highly trained and experienced in military tactics. The Continental Army had experience only in small skirmishes with the Native Americans and on the side of the British during the French and Indian War. The colonies also had little money to equip the Continental Army.

In addition to fighting the British, the Revolutionaries had to fight forces within the country who continued to be loyal to the king. Some loyalists were passive and merely refused to fight for the colonists. Others furnished food and shelter to the British Army and some actually fought on the British side.

The Patriots, however, were fighting for a cause in which they believed: their freedom. This reason was powerful and put them at an advantage against the British Army composed of soldiers who were forced to fight. The British officers were in many cases overconfident and the overconfidence caused them to blunder. The Patriots were helped to an extent by freedom-loving people from other lands. The French government was particularly helpful by sending money, supplies, soldiers, and ships. Marquis de Lafayette and Baron de Kalb were among the volunteers from France.

Match these vocabulary words with their definition.

2.22 _____ draft

2.23 _____ self-determination

2.24 _____ precipitate

a. to decide something by one's own free will

b. to bring on or hasten

c. to make a preliminary plan

Complete these statements.

2.25 The purpose of the document titled "Declaration of the Causes and Necessity of Taking up Arms" was to _____

_____

_____ .

2.26 The reason representatives decided to write the Declaration of Independence was because

_____

_____

_____ .

2.27 The bold new idea expressed in the Declaration of Independence was that the people had

a. _____ not necessarily granted by their b. _____ .

Match the items with the best possible description.

2.28	_____	Hessians	**a.** Frenchman who fought for the colonists
2.29	_____	Olive Branch Petition	**b.** foreign mercenaries
2.30	_____	"Common Sense"	**c.** wrote Declaration of Independence
2.31	_____	Richard Henry Lee	**d.** document stating why colonists were fighting in Boston
2.32	_____	Thomas Jefferson	**e.** directed by Virginia colonists to present a resolution of independence
2.33	_____	Lafayette	**f.** booklet advocating independence from Britain

Significant Battles. Among the significant battles of the Revolutionary War was the battle of New York in July, 1776. Because the king wanted a quick end to the war, he sent a large British force to New York. General Howe was able to defeat Washington twice in New York. Then as Washington crossed the Hudson River to defend a fort in New Jersey, General Cornwallis came after him and Washington retreated for the security of Pennsylvania.

The battles of Trenton and Princeton were also important. In December of 1776, as both the British and the Patriots were preparing to cease fighting for the winter, Washington saw his opportunity to be victorious through a surprise attack. On Christmas night Washington crossed the Delaware River to find the Hessians (hired German soldiers) celebrating the holidays. Washington captured the Hessians with scarcely a shot being fired. In the meantime, Cornwallis, who had received word of the capture, came down from New York. Washington slipped around Cornwallis and attacked. Washington's victories restored Patriot confidence in the effort.

British General John Burgoyne was commissioned to conduct a march through New York later. Because Washington was following Howe through Pennsylvania, Burgoyne seemingly could not be stopped. After Burgoyne captured the American force at Fort Ticonderoga, he marched toward the Hudson River. Americans slowed his progress by cutting down trees and putting them in his path. In addition, the Green Mountain Boys closed in behind Burgoyne and threatened his supply lines. As Burgoyne continued his delayed march, General Horatio Gates was busily forming an army to stop him. Gates stationed his army on Bemis Heights with a river on one side and the woods on the other.

Fierce fighting lasted ten days and finally ended at Saratoga with Burgoyne surrendering his entire British army. British General Howe managed to capture Philadelphia in 1777, however, the city offered little military advantage. It was only a comfortable city in which to spend the winter. Even though capture of the capital city usually means the end of the war, it did not in this case. The Continental Congress merely left Philadelphia and held congressional sessions in Lancaster, Pennsylvania.

While the British forces enjoyed a comfortable winter in Philadelphia, the Patriots suffered the severe cold at Valley Forge where they were coached in military tactics by Baron von Steuben, a captain in the German army. The Patriots learned that winter how to fight in a more professional manner.

In December of 1777, the British Army won a decisive battle in Savannah, Georgia. This action caused Congress to organize a Southern army under the command of Benjamin Lincoln. Battles occurred for a year until British commander Henry Clinton defeated Lincoln in Charleston. The loss of Lincoln's army was America's biggest defeat of the war. The Americans were later victorious in battles in North Carolina and in South Carolina under Nathaniel Greene.

Most fighting in the West involved the Native American groups who were threatened by the British with loss of their hunting grounds if the colonists won the war. George Rogers Clark decided to focus on ending the Native American attacks; therefore, he led a force of Patriots down the Ohio River. He was able to capture British frontier forts in what is now Illinois and Indiana. Clark's victories gave the Americans a hold on the West and the Native Americans became less of a threat.

Fighting raged at sea also. The American navy was small and relatively inexperienced, but it was generally successful. The most famous sea battle of the Revolution was between a British man-of-war and a ship under the command of John Paul Jones. As he sailed in the Atlantic, Jones encountered a fleet of British supply ships guarded by warships. Jones attacked the largest warship and during the three-hour battle his ship, the *Bonhomme Richard*, suffered severe damage. When the British commander called out, "Have you lowered your flag?" Jones replied in the famous words, "I have not yet begun to fight!" The battle continued and the British ship finally surrendered. Jones had proved that the Americans could fight at sea as well as on land.

The battle of Yorktown signaled the end of the Revolutionary War. That battle was **precipitated** by defeats for Cornwallis in the south. As Cornwallis awaited additional troops in Yorktown, Lafayette wrote to Washington that he should bring his main army south before the relief ships arrived. French forces commanded by Admiral De Grasse and Lafayette combined with the American forces outside of Yorktown and battled to a stand-off with the British relief forces. Cornwallis had no choice but to surrender. The fighting was essentially over. General Nathaniel Greene had control of the southern colonies. The British held only New York and Charleston, which they later evacuated. In December of 1782 the first articles of peace were signed.

Write the correct letter for the answer on the line.

2.34 What was a significant event for this battle? The fall of New York: _____

a. The battle signaled the end of the Revolutionary War.
b. Colonists cut down trees to slow Burgoyne's progress to Saratoga where he lost his entire army.
c. Washington was defeated twice by a large British Army.
d. Even though it was the capital city, it did not mean the end of the war. It provided British with comfortable quarters.
e. Washington surprised the Hessians on Christmas Eve while they were celebrating.

2.35 What was a significant event for this battle? The battles of Trenton and Princeton: _____

a. The battle signaled the end of the Revolutionary War.
b. Colonists cut down trees to slow Burgoyne's progress to Saratoga where he lost his entire army.
c. Washington was defeated twice by a large British Army.
d. Even though it was the capital city, it did not mean the end of the war. It provided British with comfortable quarters.
e. Washington surprised the Hessians on Christmas Eve while they were celebrating.

2.36 What was a significant event for this battle? Burgoyne's march through New York: _____

a. The battle signaled end of Revolutionary War.
b. Colonists cut down trees to slow Burgoyne's progress to Saratoga where he lost his entire army.
c. Washington was defeated twice by a large British Army.
d. Even though it was the capital city, it did not mean the end of the war. It provided British with comfortable quarters.
e. Washington surprised the Hessians on Christmas Eve while they were celebrating.

2.37 What was a significant event for this battle? The capture of Philadelphia: _____

a. The battle signaled end of Revolutionary War.
b. Colonists cut down trees to slow Burgoyne's progress to Saratoga where he lost his entire army.
c. Washington was defeated twice by a large British Army.
d. Even though it was the capital city, it did not mean the end of the war. It provided British with comfortable quarters.
e. Washington surprised the Hessians on Christmas Eve while they were celebrating.

2.38 What was a significant event for this battle? The battle of Yorktown: _____

a. The battle signaled end of Revolutionary War.
b. Colonists cut down trees to slow Burgoyne's progress to Saratoga where he lost his entire army.
c. Washington was defeated twice by a large British Army.
d. Even though it was the capital city, it did not mean the end of the war. It provided British with comfortable quarters.
e. Washington surprised the Hessians on Christmas Eve while they were celebrating.

COLONIAL GOVERNMENT

In anticipation of an American victory in the Revolutionary War, the Second Continental Congress had already begun to establish a central government for the colonies. Individual states had also begun to develop state governments after the Declaration of Independence was written. Many of the colonies wrote state constitutions similar to their charters, but government powers were limited.

All state constitutions provided qualifications for holding office and for voting. Many constitutions provided for the separation of church and state so that the government could not establish a state church. All the states except Georgia banned the importing of slaves; and the Northern states gradually declared emancipation for slaves. Many states provided for public schools in their constitutions and Massachusetts maintained its constitutional law which required public support of education.

Articles of Confederation. In 1776, the Second Continental Congress appointed a committee to draft a national constitution. By 1781, all states had ratified the Articles of Confederation. This constitution was a loose confederation that lacked strong, centralized powers. Among the weaknesses of the Articles were equal voting powers, which caused disputes between large and small states. Congress was given the power to levy taxes, but it could not collect them. As a result, the government never had enough money. Congress also lacked power to control trade and commerce between states and nations. Also, no system of courts existed in which to try violators of national laws.

The weaknesses in the Articles of Confederation ultimately led to their revision. A dispute between Virginia and Maryland over the Potomac River rights convinced Congress that it had no power to settle such fights. The arguing states sent delegates to attempt to settle the dispute. Congress recommended in February of 1787 that all the states send delegates to Philadelphia for a convention to revise the Articles of Confederation. During this convention, the Constitution of the United States was drafted.

The Articles of Confederation lasted for only two years, but they did serve a purpose. They represented the government that brought the Revolutionary War to an end. They brought independence to the people and established a peace. They also provided the framework that kept the states together. The Articles were weak; however, they provided the basis for stronger government in the future.

Complete these activities.

2.39   To stop or refuse to do something is to _____ .

2.40   To be protected from something is to be _____ .

2.41   What were four weaknesses of the Articles of Confederation?

a. _____

_____

b. _____

_____

c. _____

_____

d. _____

_____

Constitution of the United States. The convention for the revision of the Articles of Confederation began by electing George Washington chairman and by agreeing to conduct all meetings in private without news releases or progress reports.

Two plans were suggested at the convention. One was the Virginia Plan proposed by Edmund Randolf. He suggested that a national government be established consisting of three branches: executive, judiciary, and legislative. Randolf's proposal meant that the articles would be completely rewritten rather than revised. In the Virginia Plan the Congress would consist of two houses in which the total number of delegates would be divided among the states on the basis of the free population of each state. An executive would be selected by Congress and a system of national courts would be established. Under the Virginia Plan, the states with the greatest population would control Congress. The smaller states **balked** at that part of the plan. William Paterson of New Jersey presented an alternative proposal called the New Jersey Plan, which called for a one-house legislature in which each state would cast only one vote. This action caused the larger states to balk; they would lose power with the New Jersey Plan.

A compromise committee was appointed to solve the problem. That committee suggested a two-house legislature composed of a House of Representatives and a Senate.

The House would be allotted votes on the basis of population and the Senate would have equal representation. That compromise is now referred to as "The Great Compromise."

Various recommendations about the executive branch of the government were proposed. Some delegates to the convention suggested an executive committee rather than one individual as head of the executive branch. Some wanted the executive to serve until death; others preferred that person to serve for only one year. Some thought the executive should be appointed by Congress, others thought he should be elected by popular vote. Finally, the delegates decided to have one person as the executive, to have his term in office four years, and to have him chosen by the electors. Judges of federal courts would be appointed by the executive, or president. Congress was given powers to regulate commerce among the states and with foreign countries.

By September of 1787, the outline of the Constitution was complete. None of the delegates was completely satisfied with every part of the Constitution, but all were generally pleased with it. The Constitution needed ratification by all the states. Those who favored the Constitution were known as Federalists and those who opposed it were known as Antifederalists.

Ratification of the Constitution did not come swiftly or easily. Some states worried that the federal government would become too strong and too powerful under the Constitution. Virginia was one of these states, but Virginia finally agreed to ratify the Constitution when it was promised that a Bill of Rights would be written immediately. Some states were persuaded to ratify the Constitution by George Washington who promised to be the first president. Finally, in 1790, all states had ratified the document.

The Constitution of the United States is unique in government history and has survived because of several important features. It divides power between the federal government, the states, and the local governments. The central government receives its powers from the people and is answerable to the people.

The Constitution, through its three branches of government, has a system of checks and balances. The president can check Congress by vetoing legislation, Congress can check the president by overriding the veto, and the Supreme Court can check Congress through judicial review. The system may, as some

Confederation ᵛˢ Constitution

Loose union of states; no strong executive head.	Close-knit union of states; strong executive head.
Congress could levy, but not collect taxes.	Power to levy taxes.
No power to regulate trade between states and foreign nations.	Power to regulate interstate and foreign commerce.

have charged, slow government; but political power is prevented from dominating any one branch of the government.

The Constitution can also be amended. The Congress, by a two-thirds vote of both houses, may submit an amendment to the state legislatures for ratification. Another means of amending the Constitution is by calling a Constitutional Convention. This latter method has not been used since the document was first written.

Complete the following.

2.42 The convention for revision of the Articles of Confederation elected as chairman:

_____

2.43 In the Virginia Plan, the two houses of Congress would be populated:

_____

2.44 Edmund Randolf suggested that a government be established consisting of three branches:

_____

2.45 William Paterson suggested an alternate to the Virginia Plan that was called:

_____

2.46 The result of "The Great Compromise" was:

_____

_____

2.47 One of the important features of the Constitution is that:

_____

_____

Federal Government. Under its new Constitution, the federal government of the United States began governing with thirteen states and a population of four million people. The Congress had asked each state to elect presidential electors to the electoral college.

George Washington was elected the first president by a unanimous vote, and John Adams was elected vice president. Washington was a popular president because of his careful decision making and his ability to stand firm after he had made a decision. Although no provision for a presidential cabinet was in the Constitution, Washington appointed heads of various departments and by doing so, set a precedent. Washington established departments of foreign affairs, the treasury, and war. He also appointed an Attorney General who was responsible for the legal matters of government. Washington's cabinet consisted of Alexander Hamilton, secretary of the treasury; Henry Knox, secretary of war; Thomas Jefferson, secretary of state; and Edmund Randolf, attorney general.

A Supreme Court consisting of a chief justice and five associate justices was established by the Judiciary Act of 1789. The Supreme Court was empowered to review state laws and state court decisions that involved the Constitution, treaties, or federal laws.

The first ten amendments to the Constitution—the Bill of Rights—was adopted by Congress in 1789. The Bill of Rights guaranteed individual rights to American citizens. They were ratified within two years and erased the fears of the Antifederalists.

The main problem the government faced was debt from the war and a method for new funding. Alexander Hamilton was chosen to solve the problem and in 1790 presented a financial program to Congress. Hamilton's first concern was the payment of the debts. He proposed the issuance of government bonds at an interest rate of six percent that would be offered in exchange for paper money and other debt certificates. He also proposed that the government assume the debts of the states fighting the war. Opposition to Hamilton's plan arose. Some states had already paid their war debts and they thought that other states should be obligated to pay. Paper money issued during the Revolution was now worthless. Madison also opposed Hamilton's plan and forced a compromise. In exchange for congressional approval of assuming state debts, he agreed that the national capitol be moved to Philadelphia for ten years while a permanent capitol was being built on the Potomac River.

Hamilton further proposed a plan for operating the government and suggested that government expenses be paid from income taxes. He also recommended excise taxes, particularly on distilled liquor. He also proposed a Bank of the United States, a national system of banking. The system would have a large central bank with branches in major cities, would be chartered by Congress, and would be an agent of the treasury. The bank would also issue money backed by gold reserves. Washington approved the plan and signed the bank bill into law.

Another one of Hamilton's suggestions was the establishing of metal currency. In 1792, on Hamilton's recommendation, Congress passed the Mint Act of 1792 which provided for the minting of gold, silver, and copper coins and established the decimal system of money.

Political parties rose out of the controversy between Hamilton and Madison. Jefferson and Madison became known as Democratic-Republicans, or simply Republicans. The name suggested that members of that party were the true defenders of the republic. People who agreed with Hamilton called themselves Federalists to indicate that they were not Antifederalists.

Although the nation was new, it was not **immune** from foreign policy problems. The first such problem was the French Revolution. Although many Americans were enthusiastic about the revolution, the governmental leaders decided that America was too weak to become involved and so remained neutral. America still believed it had the right to trade with warring nations. That declaration caused problems.

One problem was the seizure and search of American ships by the British. The British still occupied forts in the northwestern part of the United States because Americans had refused to pay war debts and the British enjoyed the profit from the fur trade there.

Washington decided to settle things with the British by sending John Jay to Britain to work out an agreement. Jay was able to obtain an agreement, called Jay's Treaty, that said that the British should turn over the forts along the Great Lakes to the United States. The British did not, however, agree to stop searching American ships.

The treaty was the first use of negotiations by the United States to settle a dispute and was instrumental in settling a longtime land dispute with Spain.

Spain feared that the United States would threaten the safety of Spanish Florida or Louisiana now that it had settled with Britain. The Pinckney Treaty with Spain quieted these fears. It set the United States' southern boundary and guaranteed navigation rights on the Mississippi River to American citizens. The treaty also allowed American goods to be transferred at New Orleans without payment of duties.

Match the following items.

2.48	_____	George Washington
2.49	_____	John Adams
2.50	_____	Bill of Rights
2.51	_____	Alexander Hamilton
2.52	_____	John Jay
2.53	_____	Pinckney's Treaty

a. first vice president of the United States

b. worked out a treaty with Britain

c. first president of the United States

d. treaty with Spain that clarified boundary and navigation disputes

e. first ten amendments to the Constitution

f. established a national banking system

Put a check beside the correct answer(s).

2.54 Which departments did George Washington establish as cabinet posts?

_____ foreign affairs

_____ treasury

_____ war

_____ vice president

_____ attorney general

_____ the Supreme Court

2.55 Which act established the Supreme Court?

_____ Proclamation Act

_____ Judiciary Act

_____ Navigation Act

_____ Mint Act

2.56   What were three of Hamilton's suggestions in his financial program?

_____   that states assume the debts of federal government

_____   National Bank

_____   government to be paid without using income taxes

_____   excise taxes

_____   trade with warring nations

_____   the issuance of government bonds

2.57   What were the names of two political parties that emerged during Washington's term as president?

_____

_____

2.58   The United States remained neutral during the French Revolution because the American Army was

too _____ to participate in the war.

↻ **Review the material in this section in preparation for the Self Test.** The Self Test will check your mastery of this particular section as well as your knowledge of the previous section.

SELF TEST 2

Answer *true* **or** *false* (each answer, 1 point).

2.01 _____ The first Navigation Act required that all ships carrying goods between Britain and America be British-built or owned.

2.02 _____ Thomas Jefferson was a member of the Federalist political party.

2.03 _____ The French and Indian War resulted in Britain becoming the leading colonial power in the world.

2.04 _____ The Virginia Resolves condemned the Stamp Act and said that only the colonial government should levy taxes.

2.05 _____ Writs of Assistance gave British officials the right to enter and confiscate anything the owner could not prove was smuggled.

2.06 _____ The British employed French soldiers to assist them during the early battles of the Revolutionary War.

2.07 _____ The Second Continental Congress was responsible for the writing and the adoption of the Declaration of Independence.

Complete these statements (each answer, 3 points).

2.08 The French and Indian War settled the question of

_____ .

2.09 The Hat Act of 1732 and the Iron Act of 1759 were examples of Britain's attempts to

_____ .

2.010 The Proclamation Act of 1763 restricted the freedom of the colonists to

_____ .

2.011 One of the criticisms of the Articles of Confederation was that it did not provide for

_____ .

2.012 Controversy between the Virginia Plan and the New Jersey Plan of congressional representation was settled

_____ .

2.013 One of the important features of the Constitution of the United States is that

_____

_____ .

2.014 The publication by Thomas Paine that caused colonists to think seriously about declaring

independence from Britain was named _____ .

2.015   After the Stamp Act was repealed, the British proposed a series of taxes on other goods, but the

colonists retaliated by _____ British goods.

2.016   The battle that ended the Revolutionary War was the battle of _____ .

Put a check beside the correct answer(s) (each answer, 1 point).

2.017   What were the four major points of Hamilton's plan for a sound financial program for the United
States?

_____   that states assume the debts of federal government

_____   establish a national bank system

_____   government to be paid without using income taxes

_____   place excise taxes on certain goods for government operating money

_____   government assume states' war debts

_____   trade with warring nations

_____   establish a method of issuing of government bonds

2.018   What four events led to the Revolutionary War?

_____   Declaration of Independence

_____   Stamp Act

_____   Pinckney Treaty

_____   Judiciary Act

_____   Intolerable Acts

_____   the Virginia Plan

_____   fighting in Boston

Match the following (each answer, 2 points).

2.019 _____ General Edward Braddock

2.020 _____ Patrick Henry

2.021 _____ Thomas Jefferson

2.022 _____ Richard Henry Lee

2.023 _____ Marquis de Lafayette

2.024 _____ General John Burgoyne

2.025 _____ John Paul Jones

2.026 _____ Edmund Randolf

2.027 _____ John Adams

2.028 _____ Alexander Hamilton

2.029 _____ George Washington

a. set government precedents not covered in the Constitution

b. British general during the French and Indian War

c. wrote the first financial plan for the United States

d. most vocal colonist against the Stamp Act of 1765

e. first Vice President of the United States

f. wrote the Declaration of Independence

g. suggested the Constitution allow for three branches of government

h. proposed a resolution for independence at the Second Continental Congress

i. conducted one of the most successful naval battles of the Revolutionary War

j. French soldier who fought with the colonists in the Revolutionary War

k. led unsuccessful march through New York during Revolutionary War

$\frac{51}{64}$ **SCORE** _____   ✓ **CHECK** _____   _____
   Teacher   Date

3. UNITED STATES OF THE 1800s

The 1800s provided more challenges for the new United States government. The era opened with political conflicts and controversies about the principles of nationalism and sectionalism. Disputes over slavery were prevalent during the mid-1800s and those disputes culminated with the Civil War between the North and the South. Two other wars were fought during the 1800s: the War of 1812 and the Spanish-American War. The best known statesmen in United States history, Jefferson, Monroe, Jackson, and Lincoln, were elected presidents during the era.

The 1800s proved that the immature country had become a powerful nation and was forced to deal with sophisticated problems.

Section Objectives

Review these objectives. When you have completed this section, you should be able to:

8. Explain the administrations of Presidents Jefferson, Monroe, Jackson, and Lincoln.

9. List the causes and results of the War of 1812, the Civil War, and the Spanish-American War.

10. Explain the causes of slavery.

11. Describe the Reconstruction period in the South.

Vocabulary

Study these words to enhance your learning success in this section.

deem . . . . To think or believe.

devastate . . . . To destroy; to ruin.

initiate . . . . To introduce or to begin.

ravage . . . . To destroy.

sectionalism . . . . A special interest or devotion to a certain region.

JEFFERSON TO JACKSON

Conflict existed within political parties that surrounded Thomas Jefferson's election to the presidency. The Federalist Party was worried because the Republican Party was rapidly gaining new members, many of whom were immigrants. The Federalists, therefore, decided to make an issue of the continuing quarrels with France as a means of restricting the Republicans. Federalists forced four measures through Congress. One of those measures was the Naturalization Act, which required that a foreigner live in the United States for fourteen years before he could become a citizen and vote. Another measure was the Alien Act which permitted the president to deport aliens **deemed** "dangerous to the peace and safety of the United States." Another act, the Alien Enemies Act, allowed the president to imprison or to deport dangerous aliens in war time. The fourth act was the Sedition Act, which authorized fines of up to $5,000 and imprisonment for up to five years for anyone who tried to hinder the operation of the government.

The controversy over the Alien and Sedition Acts, as they were called, lost the Federalist Party many members. Citizens of the United States even became critical of other Federalist programs, such as Hamilton's financial policy, the growing centralization of government, increased taxes, and failure to reduce the nation's debt.

As a result, the Federalist candidates lost the election of 1800. The two Republican candidates, Thomas Jefferson and Aaron Burr, each received seventy-three votes in the electoral college and the House of Representatives was forced to make the decision of who would be president. The Federalists in the House could throw the election either way. Although Hamilton, the power of the Federalist Party, disliked Jefferson, he realized that Burr was unprincipled; so, he influenced the other Federalists to vote for Jefferson. Jefferson was elected.

Jefferson referred to his election as "The Revolution of 1800." He believed that the strength of a government is based upon its popularity and not upon its force. One of his first acts as president was to free people who had been imprisoned because of the Sedition Act.

Jefferson did not, however, make wide changes in the government. He kept many Federalist office-holders on his staff and continued the Bank of the United States. He did advocate a government that

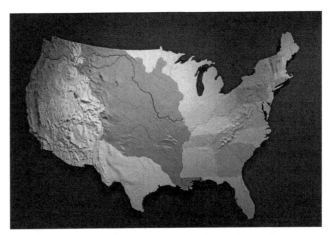

| The Louisiana Purchase added much territory to the United States.

was open to honest, intelligent, and educated people. As his administration progressed, his concern for the common citizen gained support. States with property ownership restrictions for voting began to change those laws and to adopt suffrage. Jefferson did not want people burdened with government. He eliminated all internal excise taxes and increased government income through customs duties and the sale of lands in the West. Jefferson also reduced the army and sold navy vessels to save money.

Marbury versus Madison. *Marbury v. Madison* was an important case because it established the principle that the Supreme Court could declare acts of Congress unconstitutional. The case involved William Marbury, one of the judges appointed by former President John Adams before he left office. Marbury had not been granted his commission of office before Jefferson took office. Marbury asked the Supreme Court to force Secretary of State James Madison to give him his commission. Chief Justice John Marshall, realizing that another political party battle could occur because Marbury was a Federalist and Madison was a Republican, decided that the court could not review the case. The Court was powerless to force Madison to grant the commission because of a conflict between the Constitution and the Judiciary Act of 1789. Marshall declared that part of the Judiciary Act unconstitutional.

Louisiana Purchase. The Louisiana Purchase was motivated by the closing of the port of New Orleans to American trade and traffic. The closing of the port was the result of the continuing war between France and Britain. Spain became an ally of France and secretly gave Louisiana to France to hold until after the war. Jefferson learned about the secret deal and sent James Monroe to France to buy New Orleans from Napoleon. In the meantime, Napoleon, who desperately needed money for the war, called on Robert Livingston, the United States minister in Paris. Napoleon offered to sell all of the land drained by the Mississippi and Missouri rivers. By the time Monroe arrived, the price of the land had been set at $15 million, more than Monroe had been authorized to pay. Monroe and Livingston decided to buy the land anyway to Jefferson's later delight.

Jefferson, however, was worried because the Constitution does not authorize the president to buy foreign land. As predicted, Federalists from New England opposed the purchase. They were concerned that the new territory would further weaken their influence. The Senate, however, approved the treaty with France and the House of Representatives approved the money to execute the purchase.

Complete these statements.

3.1 The vocabulary word which means *a special interest or devotion to a certain region* is

_____ .

3.2 The vocabulary word meaning *to think* or *believe* is _____ .

3.3 *Marbury v. Madison* established the principle that _____

_____ .

3.4 Jefferson referred to his election as _____ .

3.5 To reduce the burden of government, Jefferson _____

_____ .

3.6 Jefferson's Republican opponent in the 1800 election in the House of Representatives was

_____ .

3.7 As a result of Jefferson's concern about government for the common citizen, many states passed

laws that _____ .

3.8 Negotiations with France to purchase Louisiana were motivated by

_____ .

3.9 Jefferson chose _____ to negotiate the Louisiana Purchase.

WAR OF 1812

The War of 1812 was a war over the honor of the new United States. It drew the U.S. to fight Britain again while that nation was fighting the French emperor, Napoleon. The war was also one of miscommunication and misunderstanding.

Causes of the war. Napoleon was bent on destroying British trade with Europe. In retaliation, Great Britain issued the Orders in Council, which declared a blockade of French ports and other ports under French control. This hurt U.S. trade. Although the United States had not expected to suffer from the conflict between Britain and France, it did. The United States had been making money from the European war by trading with both sides. The United States would lose huge profits from trading only with Britain and neutral nations. Thus, the new blockade angered the Americans as did the British habit of impressing, or taking, U.S. sailors to man their warships.

An Embargo Act passed in 1807 closed all American ports to all foreign ships and stopped American ships from sailing for any foreign ports. The Embargo Act was designed to hurt Great Britain, but it hurt the United States instead. Overseas trade all but stopped and goods piled up in warehouses. The Macon Act of 1810 removed restrictions on trade. It said that the United States would stop trading with either France or Britain if the country would not change its trading policy.

Finally, President James Madison on June 1, 1812, asked Congress to declare war on Great Britain. His reasons were the continued impressment of United States sailors, the interference with United States trade, and the British inciting Native American warfare in the Northwest.

First, the United States invaded Canada hoping to drive the British out. That attempt failed. After Napoleon's defeat in Europe, Britain was able to send additional troops to America. After many battles, the British Army occupied Washington, D.C. and burned the Capitol, the White House, and other buildings. Nevertheless, the British were unable to hold the city. The last battle of the war was the battle of New Orleans which was actually fought after the treaty was signed in Europe. A treaty was signed in Ghent on December 24, 1814, with terms that all land captured during the war be given up. All was to be exactly as it had been before the war.

Results of the war. One important result of the war was the increase in American manufacturing that occurred because of it. During the war, people were unable to import goods from Britain and began making many articles for themselves. In addition, many of the problems that had led to the war disappeared after the war.

Andrew Jackson's and William Henry Harrison's elections to the presidency were indirect results of the war. Both had gained military fame during the war and became popular candidates for the presidency. The Federalist Party also declined in influence and in power after the war. Nationalism flourished after the war, encouraged to an extent by the War Hawks. Several flaws in the government became evident. Madison had permitted the Bank of the United States to go out of business when its charter expired creating a money problem. Problems with military supplies and transportation were also evident. The result was much national legislation to correct these problems.

| The British burned the Capitol in the War of 1812.

Answer *true* or *false*.

3.10 _____ Britain and France wanted to destroy trade between the United States and other neutral countries.

3.11 _____ The War of 1812 was actually the result of misunderstanding and miscommunication.

3.12 _____ The last battle of the War of 1812 was in Canada.

3.13 _____ Nationalism was begun by the Federalist Party.

3.14 _____ One governmental flaw that was discovered after the War of 1812 was a problem of the lack of a national bank.

MONROE ERA

James Monroe, who followed James Madison into the presidency, was swept up by the new national feeling that invaded the country after the War of 1812. Monroe coined the phrase "Era of Good Feelings" to describe the period. In addition, he toured the country, which was something no other president had done before.

Nationalism. In the spirit of the new nationalism, because British goods were flooding American markets and driving American manufacturers out of business, Congress passed a protective tariff on many imported goods. Also during the period Chief Justice John Marshall helped strengthen national government with his Supreme Court opinions. Marshall's decisions accomplished several things. His broad interpretation of the Constitution strengthened the federal government but at the expense of the states. The Supreme Court, through Marshall, gained importance in the federal government.

Monroe Doctrine. The Monroe Doctrine was delivered to Congress in December 1823 and is a landmark in United States history. The Monroe Doctrine provided that the United States should not take part in any wars or disputes which involved only European countries, that the United States would not interfere with colonies or countries dependent on Europe, that American continents are not subject for future colonization by European nations, and that Europe should not attempt to colonize in this hemisphere.

The European countries did not believe the Monroe Doctrine to be very important. They knew about the weak military of the United States and considered President Monroe's guarding of the Western Hemisphere ridiculous. However, the Europeans knew that the British Navy would back up the Monroe Doctrine; therefore, they eventually recognized United States policy. Although it was not tested at the time, the Doctrine's importance to United States foreign policy would become evident later.

Complete this activity.

3.15 What are four important events of the Monroe Era?

a. _____

b. _____

c. _____

d. _____

JACKSON ERA

Andrew Jackson's presidency was preceded by the beginnings of **sectionalism**. People living in various regions of the country developed attitudes and viewpoints that developed from their own economic interests. Politicians also developed these interests and attempted to pass legislation that favored their own sections. Several sectional attitudes were evident. The Northeast wanted higher tariffs and a national bank because that section was becoming an industrial center and needed available money. The South, on the other hand, favored low protective tariffs because that section needed import goods for cotton cultivation. That section also favored westward expansion because it needed new lands. The southerners had river transportation and they were unsympathetic to internal improvements. The West wanted land easily available for farming and the construction of roads and canals.

Another sectional issue led to the Missouri Compromise of 1820. Missouri, a slave state, asked for admittance to the Union. At the time, the United States had eleven slave states and eleven free states. Southerners insisted that Congress had no constitutional right to determine whether a state would be free or slave. The North insisted that Congress could decide. About that time, Maine asked for admittance to the Union as a free state and the Compromise allowed Missouri to enter as a slave state. However, after that the remainder of the Louisiana Territory north of Missouri's southern border was required to enter the Union as free states.

| Andrew Jackson was the founder of the Democratic Party.

Andrew Jackson's election to the presidency in 1828 did not change the conflict between those who supported sectionalism and those who supported nationalism. Jackson believed in states' rights and he supported many of the sectional views in the West. Jackson, however, would not submit to many of the sectional demands. When necessary, he asserted the federal government's power. Jackson's political philosophy was akin to that of Thomas Jefferson. He believed that the people of the United States should have a share in the government through their voting powers. In line with that philosophy, Jackson opened educational, economic, and political opportunities to the people. He also was instrumental in securing suffrage for the people by encouraging the states to further liberalize their voting requirements. Jackson was also noted for his strong nationalistic foreign policy and his belief that the states should be responsible for internal improvements, such as roads and canals.

Among Jackson's accomplishments while in office was his decision not to recharter the Bank of the United States. He replaced that bank with smaller state banks. Money problems continued to plague the government as the president of the National Bank recalled loans and refused to make new ones. As the state banks grew wealthier, they began to lend money more easily and paper money declined in value. However, the sale of Western lands was bringing in enough money to pay the national debt.

The Democratic-Republicans split into two parties under Jackson. The Whigs were more sympathetic to the North while the Democrats were sympathetic to the South and supportive of states' rights. Both parties, however, drew votes from all sections of the country.

Complete these statements.

3.16   The vocabulary word which means *to introduce* or *begin* is _____ .

3.17   Sectionalism is illustrated in the Northeast's desire for high protective tariffs because the Northeast

was a(n) _____ section of the country.

3.18   In 1820, the state that wanted to be admitted to the Union as a slave state was

_____ .

3.19   Andrew Jackson's philosophy of government might be compared to the philosophy of

_____ .

3.20   After the charter for the Bank of the United States was not renewed, Jackson established

_____ banks.

Answer *true* **or** *false*.

3.21   _____   Jackson was noted for his strong nationalistic foreign policy.

3.22   _____   Because of money gained from sale of Western lands, the government was able to
pay the national debt.

3.23   _____   Jackson was not in favor of suffrage for the people.

3.24   _____   Jackson opened educational, economic, and political opportunities for the people.

3.25   _____   The state that requested entrance to the union as a free state in 1820 was
Massachusetts.

3.26   _____   The Democratic-Republican Party split into the Whigs and the Democrats.

SLAVERY: ORIGINS AND DISPUTES

Events of the mid-1800s relate directly and indirectly to slavery. The United States expansion into the West brought questions of whether slaves might be taken by their owners into those sections of the country. Another dispute was whether new states would be admitted to the Union as slave or free states. In addition, the attitudes of people about what was right for their particular section of the country caused debate and was a consideration in any discussion about slavery.

Origin of Slavery. Slaves were brought to this country as early as 1619 when twenty black servants landed in Jamestown. From that point until 1865, black people were brought to this country to work as laborers. As time passed, more and more black people lived their entire lives in slavery. As fewer indentured servants and Native Americans were

available for field labor, more and more black people were brought to do the work. Enslaved people were particularly valuable to colonial farmers and plantation owners. Ship owners **initiated** a slave-trade cycle known as the Atlantic Triangle in which European goods were traded for slaves in Africa. The trade was banned in the U.S. after 1807, but continued illegally until the Civil War.

Slaves were owned in all thirteen states up until the Revolution. During the American Revolutionary War, enslaved people fought for the colonies and some were freed in return for their military service. The northern states banned slavery within their borders around that time.

Economics of Slavery. An economic factor was related to slavery. In the South, slaves were important workers in the cotton fields. With the invention of the cotton gin, the cotton crops of plantation owners were expanded to keep up with the demand and the need for slaves to pick the cotton became greater.

Politics of Slavery. Slavery had been questioned almost from its onset. Benjamin Franklin was president of the first antislavery organization. George Washington and Thomas Jefferson freed their slaves in their wills. In the 1830s, new abolitionists began to speak and to write about the moral implications of slavery and racial discrimination. Such writers as William Lloyd Garrison, Theodore Dwight Weld, Harriet Beecher Stowe, and Sojourner Truth were vocal in their views against slavery. Southerners were angered by the abolitionists' outspokenness and called for their arrest.

The Underground Railroad was a network of routes for escape by runaway slaves seeking freedom in the North. Approximately fifty thousand slaves escaped to the North by this method.

Southern support for slavery increased during the time the abolitionists were most vocal. Southerners defended slavery as necessary for the economic survival of the South. Moreover, according to William Harper, the southern social order was based on slavery.

Laws of Slavery. Certain laws pertaining to slaves called slave codes were in force until just before the Civil War. They enforced the belief that enslaved people were property and should be protected by the public. The slave codes prohibited enslaved people from owning property and from testifying in court.

Write the letter of the correct answer on each line.

3.27   Slave codes prohibited enslaved people from _____ .

a. getting married   b. being sold   c. owning property   d. going to church

3.28   When they first came to the United States, slaves were used as _____ .

a. laborers   b. freedmen   c. land owners   d. citizens

3.29   More and more black slaves were brought to the United States to do field labor when _____ .

a. industrialization began in the North

c. fewer Native Americans and indentured servants were available

d. the Civil War began

3.30   A slave-trade cycle initiated by ship owners was known as _____ .

a. slave buying   b. the Atlantic Triangle   c. the Force Act   d. hiring out

3.31   Some enslaved people who fought in the Revolutionary War were _____ .

a. given promotions within the military   b. given free land and supplies

c. freed in return for their military service   d. sent back home to Africa

SECTIONALISM

Sectionalism actually began early in the 1800s with regional conflict over the National Bank, the protective tariff, and slavery. The people who lived in various regions of the country had definite opinions about the way a particular issue would effect their region. Manifest Destiny was the popular idea of the time. It meant that the United States had a God-given right to extend its way of life from the Atlantic Ocean to the Pacific Ocean. Nothing could stop the settlement of these lands. As people practiced Manifest Destiny and settled land to the south, the north, the west, and the northwest, sectionalism became more pronounced. The common person had a say in the affairs of government and was concerned about the effect of legislation on their region and the way they lived.

Life varied from region to region. In the East, temperatures fluctuated greatly providing a short growing season, so most people lived and worked in cities. The many rivers provided power to run machinery in the factories. Many immigrants settled in the northern cities where they could find work in factories. Residents of the cities invented machines and products to make work easier. The cities of the North were modern for the time. They had cobblestone streets, sidewalks, and gutters to carry sewage. Shops were run by craftsmen, printers, and grocers. People rode in horse drawn carriages and had many foods and conveniences. They lived in well-built houses and children attended public or religious schools. In some areas tenement houses were built for factory workers. The people had time to think about politics and the needs of those around them and started some of the great reform movements of the time. The Northeast was generally in favor of governmental aid to business, protective tariffs, and controlled bank credit.

The Western region encompassed a large area roughly from Ohio to Indiana to the Pacific coast. The growing season was long and the rich land was ideal for large family farms. The growing season in the northern part of the Western region was much shorter. The Southwest had less rain. In both sections cattle and sheep were raised. Houses in the West were log cabins or houses made of sod in the open prairie. Mountain areas yielded precious metals. The West generally attracted people who were adventurous. Rigid class distinctions, like those in the East and South, were absent. The people of the West wanted internal improvements financed by the government, cheap or free public land, and bank credit. They were also opposed to slavery.

| Cotton was the primary reason for slavery in the South.

The South was rural and farming was the main occupation. Southerners raised cotton, tobacco, rice, sugar, and hemp. Most people lived on small farms or on large plantations. City dwellers were employed in commerce that was a direct result of slave labor. Homes of plantation dwellers were large, but most people lived in small wooden or brick homes. Cities such as Atlanta and New Orleans were as modern in appearance as those in the North. A distinct class structure dominated the South. At the top of the structure were planters, cotton growers, and tobacco magnates. The next level consisted of trained professionals such as doctors, lawyers, teachers, and the clergy. At the next level were small independent farmers, merchants, and white craftsmen. The poor white people and the enslaved people were at the bottom of the structure. Slavery was the most important factor that separated the South from the rest of the nation.

Complete these statements.

3.32   The South was rural and _____ was the main occupation of Southerners.

3.33   _____ was the most important factor that separated the South from the rest of the nation.

CIVIL WAR

In 1860, four candidates ran for the office of president. Stephen Douglas, who had failed to be nominated at the Democratic convention, ran without support from the South. The South subsequently nominated John Breckenridge, who supported federal protection of slavery in the territories. The Republican Party nominated Abraham Lincoln, who was, at that time, more moderate on slavery. The fourth candidate was John Bell of Tennessee whose Constitutional Union Party supported the Constitution and the enforcement of law. Bell made no reference to slavery.

Abraham Lincoln was elected with 40 percent of the vote and 180 electoral votes from free states, except New Jersey. Breckenridge carried all the states of the lower South. Regional politics played an important role in Abraham Lincoln's presidency, such as the South's eventual secession from the Union and the outbreak of the Civil War.

Secession of the South. A month after the election, South Carolina called a state convention. The delegates voted to repeal the state's ratification of the Constitution and to secede from the Union. Political leaders in other states urged their people to give Lincoln a chance, to wait and see if he would enforce the Fugitive Slave Law. By the beginning of 1861, Mississippi, Florida, Alabama, Georgia, Louisiana, and Texas had seceded from the Union. Several arguments made secession desirable for these states. The tariff that benefited the North and penalized the South would be ended. They thought slave trade might reopen and Cuba, Santo Domingo, or Mexico might be annexed, which would extend the plantation system.

| Abraham Lincoln faced a dividing nation.

Most Southerners were not worried about war with the North. President James Buchanan, who was still in office when the South seceded, said that secession was unconstitutional, but that Congress had no power to force the states to return to the Union. Several compromises were suggested, but all failed to be accepted.

On the same day that a compromise meeting was taking place, the six seceding states met in Montgomery, Alabama. They formed the Confederate States of America and adopted a flag. They elected Jefferson Davis president and drafted a constitution similar to the United States Constitution. The Confederate constitution, however, included provisions to restrict the new government from passing laws that interfered with slavery, from initiating protective tariffs, and from appropriating funds for internal improvements.

In his inaugural address in March of 1861, Lincoln said that he would enforce federal regulations, assist in returning fugitive slaves to all states, and maintain the Union.

Match the following items.

3.34 _____ Abraham Lincoln

3.35 _____ John Breckenridge

3.36 _____ South Carolina

3.37 _____ Jefferson Davis

3.38 _____ Alabama

3.39 _____ James Buchanan

a. southern candidate for President in 1860

b. state in which Confederation Convention was held

c. elected president in 1860

d. United States president at the time of the secession

e. first state to secede from the Union

f. president of the Confederate States of America

Outbreak of the War. The Confederacy had made military plans and had captured federal forts and buildings in the South. Major Robert Anderson at Fort Sumter reported to Lincoln that he could not defend the fort without assistance. Lincoln did not want to recognize the Confederacy, but he knew the Confederacy needed the Charleston harbor. As Anderson awaited supplies from Lincoln, General P.G.T. Beauregard ordered the attack on Fort Sumter.

After the fall of Fort Sumter, Lincoln called for volunteers to enlist in the military service and ordered a naval blockade of all ports in the South. At that point, Virginia joined the secession. Later, Arkansas, North Carolina, and Tennessee seceded, leaving Maryland, Kentucky, Missouri, and Delaware, slave states, in the Union. Every Confederate state contained counties that were sympathetic to the Union. During the Civil War, men from the South who believed in the Union fought on the Northern side and Confederate sympathizers from the North fought for the Confederacy. Even members of the same family sometimes fought on opposite sides.

Money was needed to fight the Civil War. The Morrill Tariff was passed to increase import tariffs and industrial wages, and paper money was issued. The North also sold bonds and passed the National Banking Act. Both the North and the South eventually conscripted soldiers, but the South's conscription was not successful. The South financed the war through an excise tax, by selling bonds to individuals, and by issuing paper money. Attempts by the South to borrow money from European banks were unsuccessful.

The Northern strategy was to continue the blockade of Southern ports, to capture key transportation centers along the Mississippi, to split the Confederacy by sending troops from the Mississippi across to Atlanta, and to capture the Confederate capitol in Richmond.

Both the North and the South had advantages. The North had a larger population, manufacturing interests that were greater than those in the South, vast natural resources, agricultural products available from the West, transportation via railroads, an established government, and an army and navy. The South, on the other hand, could fight a defensive war; it had only to hold its own territory and it planned to divide the Northeast from the Midwest. Southerners were united in their beliefs that they were fighting for the preservation of their way of life.

Southerners were also familiar with their climate and geography. Many Southern soldiers were West Point graduates.

One of the most successful Union plans was the Union blockade. Union ships patrolled the Atlantic and Gulf coasts preventing guns and ammunition from being imported. Other supplies could not arrive in the South and cotton could not be exported across the blockade. On one occasion, the South tried to break the blockade by sending the ironclad ship, the *Merrimack*, to attack Federal ships. The *Merrimack* was met by the Union ironclad, the *Monitor*. Neither ship was able to damage the other and the South was unable to break the blockade.

Battles of Importance. The first major battle of the Civil War was fought near Richmond at Bull Run. As the fight continued during the day, it seemed likely that the Union would win. The Union soldiers were inexperienced but they seemed to be winning until Confederate General Thomas J. Jackson took his "stonewall" stand while the Confederates drove the Union troops from the battlefield.

In the West, battles centered on forts along the Mississippi. After a series of battles the Union had gained control of the Mississippi as far as Memphis, Tennessee. Later, Federal troops captured New Orleans.

In the East the Union army continued plans to capture Richmond. General McClellan needed additional troops from Washington, but those troops were busy defending the capital from Stonewall Jackson. General Robert E. Lee met the Union army in the Seven Days battle where losses on both sides were great. The bloodiest battle of the war, however, was the battle of Antietam near Sharpsburg, Maryland. McClellan's troops attacked Lee's troops. In the one-day battle, ten thousand Confederate soldiers and twelve thousand Union soldiers lost their lives.

After the bloody battle of Antietam, Lincoln issued a preliminary Emancipation Proclamation declaring that all slaves in rebelling states would be free on January 1, 1863. The Proclamation, however, did not set one slave free nor did it shorten the war.

The battle of Chancellorsville was a victory for Lee, but Stonewall Jackson was killed there by one of his own men who mistook him for a Union scout as he returned to camp at night. The three-day battle of Gettysburg ended with the defeat of General Lee. That battle cost the lives of almost forty-six thousand men.

The Civil War

☆ Major Battles
→ Union Campaign
→ Confederate Campaign
■ Union State
■ Confederate State

Another victory for the Union was led by General Ulysses S. Grant. Vicksburg, Mississippi, was the only important city on the Mississippi that the Union had not captured although Grant had tried to capture the city five times before. He marched troops down the west side of the Mississippi. Grant was unsuccessful in that attempt but he waited, cut the city's supplies and forty-seven days later the city surrendered. Later Grant succeeded in capturing Chattanooga, an important railroad terminal.

The capture of Chattanooga gave General William T. Sherman a basis for his march to the sea. Grant had taken over command of the army of the Potomac.

He chased Lee into the South. At Cold Harbor, Grant lost many men the first month, but he decided to capture Richmond. Sherman was victorious in Atlanta and left that city to separate the lower South from the rest of the Confederacy. Sherman left death and destruction in his path to Richmond. Grant, approaching from the North, captured Lee's supply lines to Richmond. Generals Lee and Grant met at the Appomattox Court House near Richmond in April of 1865, and General Lee signed the surrender that ended the war between the states.

Answer *true* or *false*.

3.40 _____ The South passed the Morrill Tariff to raise money for the Civil War.

3.41 _____ The North planned to blockade Southern ports as part of the war strategy.

3.42 _____ In the battle of the *Monitor* and the *Merrimack*, the *Merrimack* won.

3.43 _____ General Grant surrendered to General Lee at Appomattox Court House.

3.44 _____ The bloodiest battle of the Civil War was Antietam.

RECONSTRUCTION OF THE SOUTH

After the Civil War the slaves were freed and the Union was preserved, but the South was **ravaged**. Almost all battles had been fought in the South and the land was **devastated**. The Southern people were victims of poverty and depression, and the freed slaves, numbering four million, looked to the federal government for help.

Lincoln had planned to pardon secessionists who took an oath of loyalty to the Union and emancipated the slaves. He was ready to "bind the nation's wounds." Just five days after Lee surrendered to Grant, Lincoln was assassinated as he watched a play in Ford's Theater. John Wilkes Booth, the assassin, was angered by the Confederate defeat. His senseless act slowed the progress of Reconstruction because of the bitterness felt by the Northerners at Lincoln's assassination. Andrew Johnson, Lincoln's vice president, became the next president.

Freed Slaves. The Freedman's Bureau was established by Congress in 1865 to help black people adjust to freedom and to help protect their civil rights.

After the slaves were freed, the black codes were revised. Although the codes allowed black people to swear out affidavits in criminal cases, to sue or to be sued, and to testify during a trial, black people still could not carry weapons, could not vote, hold public office, or meet in large groups. In most states black people could not work as skilled laborers and they were bound to their jobs by contract.

The Emancipation Proclamation passed during the Civil War did not go far enough in protecting the freedoms of black people. A Constitutional amendment was needed. The Thirteenth Amendment was passed and was ratified by twenty-seven states in December, 1865. It abolished slavery forever.

In 1866, Congress passed the first Civil Rights Act, which granted citizenship to all people born in the United States, except Native Americans.

In 1867, a group of Republicans calling themselves the Republican Radicals passed the first Reconstruction Act over Johnson's veto. The act divided all Confederate states into five military districts. Tennessee was excepted because it had ratified the Fourteenth Amendment. Each district was governed by an army general. The general was removed as soon as states held new constitutional conventions that included all male citizens. They then needed to draft and approve a new state constitution. The new state governments were required to guarantee the voting rights of black males and to ratify the Fourteenth Amendment.

Other reconstruction laws were passed by Congress. One measure authorized the military commanders in each region to register voters, to supervise elections, to appoint and remove state officials, and to approve simple majority for ratification of state constitutions. Reconstruction measures prevented former Confederate soldiers and officials from voting or holding political office. During that period many black men were elected to office.

Many new legislatures at that time passed laws of benefit to the South and many eliminated property qualifications for voting. Some states reapportioned their districts for state legislatures and representation in Congress. Some states abolished debtors prison and provided for free schools. Many states appropriated money for the restoration of roads, bridges, and factories in the South.

Even with the Constitutional amendments and Civil Rights acts, the participation of black people in southern government was still limited. Black people were often coerced into voting the Democratic ticket. If they did not, they found that they were not able to rent land or to receive credit in stores.

Black people were also coerced by secret organizations such as the Ku Klux Klan, Knights of the White Camellia, and the White Brotherhood. These groups physically threatened black voters and "carpetbaggers," a name given to Northerners who came south following the Civil War. In 1870, Congress passed the Force Act to protect black voters, but they were already too frightened to vote. In 1871, Congress passed the Ku Klux Klan Act to try to end the Klan's activities in southern communities.

Around that time, Northerners began to lose their interest in Reconstruction. They wondered why a few years of Reconstruction had not changed the 200-year plight of black people. Some even suggested that black people were incapable of accepting the responsibilities of citizenship. Meanwhile Democratic state legislatures passed laws that practically erased civil rights for black people. Poll taxes and literacy tests excluded both black and white people from voting until the "grandfather clause" was in effect. The grandfather clause exempted a voter from literacy tests if his grandfather was able to vote by January 1, 1860.

Economics of the South. The economic problems of the South were caused by the Confederacy's lack of capital and by the Union's seizure of cotton and other property. Extreme poverty added to the ravages of the Civil War. In addition, many white farmers lost their land to both Northern capitalists and Southern merchants. As Southern white youth grew older, they went north to find jobs in factories. The loss of Southern white youth led to the idea of the "New South" with black people working the land and white people finding jobs in factories. These ideas were the beginning of industrialization and segregation in the South.

Politics in the South. The elections of 1876 presented an electoral problem and a compromise. The Democratic candidate, Samuel Tilden, received the majority of the popular votes but only 184 electoral votes. South Carolina, Louisiana, and Florida sent in two sets of votes—one set from the carpetbag government that was still in effect. Rutherford B. Hayes needed all those votes and the votes from Oregon as well to be elected. Tilden needed only one of those votes. The confusion over the two sets of votes caused Congress to appoint an Electoral Commission containing seven Republicans, seven Democrats, and one impartial justice. The impartial justice withdrew from the commission and was replaced by a strong Republican. The Republicans voted for Rutherford B. Hayes, who became the nineteenth president.

Complete these statements.

3.45 The Freedman's Bureau was established by Congress in the year _____ .

3.46 In 1866, Congress passed the first _____ Act, which granted citizenship to all people born in the United States except Native Americans.

3.47 Poll taxes and literacy tests excluded both black and white people from voting until the

" _____ " was in effect.

SPANISH-AMERICAN WAR

As the 1800s neared their end, another war was brewing. The United States had attempted to follow the Monroe Doctrine, which stated that no European nation should interfere in the affairs of the Western continent and that the United States would not become involved in any European wars. In 1898, when the Spanish-American War broke out, the confrontation involved Cuba, only ninety miles south of Florida.

The Cubans, for years, had wanted independence from Spain. Uprisings were common and each one became more intense than the last. The United

States had invested large sums of money in Cuba over the years for railroads, refineries, and sugar plantations. Therefore, United States' interest in Cuba was great.

During the uprisings, United States' property was either damaged or destroyed. At the same time, the United States was strongly in favor of Cuban independence. Two incidents in particular intensified United States' involvement in the conflict. A letter written by the Spanish Ambassador to the United States contained remarks that insulted United States' President William McKinley. The letter was stolen and printed in a United States newspaper. The citizens were furious.

The second incident involved the battleship *Maine*, which was sent to Havana to protect United States' citizens and their property. While the *Maine* was in the harbor, it blew up and two hundred and sixty American sailors were killed. The cause of the explosion could never be determined, but the United States decided unofficially that Spain was to blame.

Congress and the United States' citizens called for a declaration of war, but President McKinley, not wanting a war, had already begun working out an agreement with Spain over Cuba. However, public opinion was overwhelming and the president asked Congress to declare war. The United States stated that its only intention was to give Cuba its independence.

The United States' fleet, under the command of Admiral George Dewey, entered Manila Bay in the Philippines, defeated the Spanish fleet and captured the city of Manila. Meanwhile, the United States' army landed in Cuba and placed the city of Santiago under siege. The Spanish fleet was then forced out of Santiago harbor toward the awaiting United States' fleet and all Spanish ships were either destroyed or captured. Theodore Roosevelt, leader of a cavalry regiment known as the Rough Riders, was victorious at the battle of San Juan Hill. That battle gave Roosevelt a later political advantage over his future opponents for the presidency.

A successful army invasion of Puerto Rico by United States' troops led by General Nelson Miles resulted in the island's capture and an end to the fighting on August 12, 1898. The peace treaty indicated a change in United States' thought about expansion, about possessions, and about international affairs.

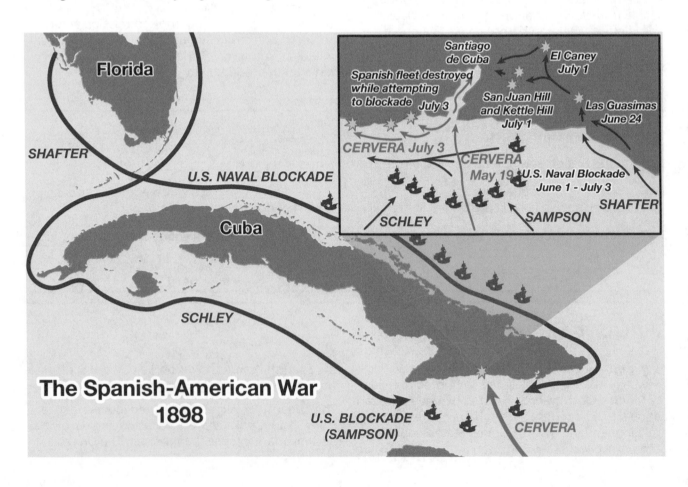

The Spanish-American War 1898

HISTORY & GEOGRAPHY 1110

LIFEPAC TEST

Name _____

Date _____

Score _____

99 / 124

Answer *true* or *false* (each answer, 1 point).

1. _____ The Crusades were an attempt by the people of Europe to recapture the Holy Land from the Muslims.

2. _____ Aaron Burr defeated Thomas Jefferson for presidency of the United States in 1880.

3. _____ During the American Revolution, Writs of Assistance gave British officials the right to enter and confiscate anything the owner could not prove was not smuggled.

4. _____ The United States' corporation system was an outgrowth of the New Deal.

5. _____ President Johnson originated civil rights legislation that was passed by Congress in 1964.

6. _____ The United States declared war on Japan because that country bombed Austria.

7. _____ The Federal Trade Commission was responsible for protecting consumers from faulty products.

8. _____ The first Navigation Act required that all ships carrying goods between Britain and America be British-built or owned.

9. _____ Chief Justice John Marshall's Supreme Court decisions helped strengthen the national government.

10. _____ Britain began colonizing in the late 1400s and early 1500s.

Write the letter of the correct answer on each line (each answer, 2 points).

11.   An invention of the Renaissance that helped sailors to accurately maneuver their ships is _____ .

a. the astrolabe   b. the sundial   c. the anchor   d. the wheel

12.   The Jamestown colony in Virginia was settled to _____ .

a. gain religious freedom for the Quakers
b. preserve the right of English Catholics to worship
c. provide raw materials for Britain
d. ensure Spain did not settle there first

13.   The French and Indian War settled the question of _____ .

a. which country controlled the North American continent
b. which country could build forts along with Great Lakes
c. which country could legally trade with the Native Americans
d. which country could legally trade with the colonies

14.   One shortcoming of the Articles of Confederation was that it did not provide for the _____ .

a. equal voting rights   b. levying of representatives
c. election of representatives   d. collection of taxes

15.   A slave-trade cycle initiated by ship owners was known as _____ .

a. slave buying   b. the Atlantic Triangle   c. hiring out   d. the Force Act

16.   In 1865, Congress established an organization to help black people adjust to freedom and to help protect their civil rights known as the _____ .

a. Emancipation Proclamation   b. Reconstruction
c. Freedman's Bureau   d. Civil Rights Program

17.   A government's desire to conquer areas beyond its border for wealth and strength is an example of _____ .

a. nationalism   b. imperialism   c. sectionalism   d. isolationism

18.   The New Deal was a set of policies that promised to _____ .

a. keep the United States out of war
b. expand the United States sphere of influence in the world
c. cure injustices within the business and financial communities
d. expand industrialization in the United States

19.   Because of the concerns of the public about pollution, Richard Nixon established _____ .

a. the Nixon Doctrine   b. the Federal Trade Commission
c. the Environmental Protection Agency   d. the New Federalism

20.   The first step in President Nixon's program of Vietnamization was _____ .

a. the bombing of North Vietnamese cities   b. the withdrawal of 25,000 servicemen
c. sending advisors to Vietnam   d. sending in additional paratroopers

Match the following (each answer, 2 points).

21. _____ John F. Kennedy
22. _____ Franklin Roosevelt
23. _____ Adolf Hitler
24. _____ Eli Whitney
25. _____ Henry Ford
26. _____ Alexander Graham Bell
27. _____ Herbert Hoover
28. _____ Lyndon Johnson
29. _____ Robert E. Lee
30. _____ Abraham Lincoln
31. _____ Ulysses S. Grant
32. _____ Johann Gutenberg
33. _____ Thomas Jefferson
34. _____ Richard Nixon
35. _____ John Smith

a. Confederate general
b. Jamestown settlement
c. Emancipation Proclamation
d. the Environmental Protection Agency
e. Union general
f. Declaration of Independence
g. printing press
h. New Frontier
i. the Great Society
j. New Deal
k. the Stock Market Crash
l. Nazi dictator
m. telephone
n. standardized parts
o. first to use an assembly line production

Complete these statements (each answer, 2 points).

36. The three classes of people in the Middle Ages were the _____ , _____ , and _____ .

37. Controversy between the Virginia Plan and the New Jersey Plan of congressional representation was settled by the _____ .

38. The scandal that rocked Richard Nixon's administration and eventually led to his resignation was the _____ scandal.

39. The Supreme Court case that established the principle that the Court could declare acts of Congress unconstitutional was _____ .

40. One of the most successful plans of the Union during the Civil War was the _____ .

41. A month after Abraham Lincoln's election to the presidency, the state of _____ seceded from the Union.

42. A network of escape routes for runaway slaves was called the _____ .

43. Woodrow Wilson was responsible for establishing an organization that would settle disagreements between nations. That organization was the _____ .

44. The president who pardoned Richard Nixon was _____ .

45. The hostages were held by Iran during the presidency of _____ .

46. President Nixon _____ because Congress was going to impeach.

47. President _____ based his foreign policy on Christian human rights.

48. Hurricane Katrina in 2005 devastated the city of _____ .

49. The terrorist attacks on _____ targeted the World Trade Center and the Pentagon.

50. The U.S. and its allies removed Saddam Hussein from power in the country of _____ .

Match the following (each answer, 2 points).

51.	_____ MacArthur	**a.**	U.S. joined World War II
52.	_____ Carter	**b.**	U.S. commander; Korea
53.	_____ cruise missile	**c.**	head of CIA
54.	_____ Menachem Begin	**d.**	peanut farmer
55.	_____ Monroe Doctrine	**e.**	no European interference in America
56.	_____ George H. W. Bush	**f.**	treaty with Egypt
57.	_____ Pearl Harbor	**g.**	preferred over the B-1 bomber
58.	_____ Thomas Paine	**h.**	invaded Kuwait
59.	_____ first space shuttle	**i.**	"Common Sense"
60.	_____ environment	**j.**	impressment of U.S. sailors
61.	_____ abortion	**k.**	Columbia
62.	_____ NAFTA	**l.**	Spanish-American War
63.	_____ Cuban independence	**m.**	control of pollution
64.	_____ War of 1812	**n.**	free trade
65.	_____ Iraq	**o.**	divisive issue

Complete these items.

3.48 The United States was initially sympathetic to Cuba's desire for independence because uprisings

occurred in favor of _____ .

3.49 What two incidents led to the Spanish-American War?

a. _____

_____

b. _____

_____

3.50 During the Spanish-American War, a change in the United States philosophy about interference in

the affairs of European nations came about because the a. _____

did interfere in the affairs of b. _____ .

Answer *true* **or** *false*.

3.51 _____ Theodore Roosevelt led the Rough Riders in an attack on San Juan Hill.

3.52 _____ President McKinley asked Congress to declare war on Cuba at the urging of his
cabinet.

3.53 _____ An investigation of the explosion of the battleship *Maine* showed that Spain was
guilty of blowing up the ship.

3.54 _____ The United States invested money in Cuba for railroads, refineries, and sugar
plantations.

3.55 _____ The last battle of the Spanish-American War was a sea battle under the command of
Admiral George Dewey.

↺ **Review the material in this section in preparation for the Self Test.** The Self Test will check your
mastery of this particular section as well as your knowledge of the previous sections.

SELF TEST 3

Answer *true* **or** *false* (each answer, 1 point).

3.01 _____ One of the measures the Republican Party forced through Congress in the early 1800s was the Naturalization Act.

3.02 _____ The Alien Enemies Act allowed the president to imprison or deport dangerous aliens in war time.

3.03 _____ Thomas Jefferson and Aaron Burr were candidates for president of the United States in 1800.

3.04 _____ In the War of 1812, the United States fought on the side of Britain.

3.05 _____ James Monroe coined the phrase "Era of Good Feelings" to describe his term as president of the United States.

3.06 _____ Chief Justice John Marshall's Supreme Court decisions helped strengthen the national government.

3.07 _____ The Missouri Compromise of 1820 allowed Maine to be admitted to the Union as a slave state.

3.08 _____ Andrew Jackson replaced the Bank of the United States with one large state bank.

3.09 _____ Slaves were brought to the United States in the early 1600s.

Write the letter of the correct answer on each line (each answer, 2 points).

3.010 A slave-trade cycle initiated by ship owners was known as _____ .

a. slave buying   b. the Force Act   c. the Atlantic Triangle   d. hiring out

3.011 A network of escape routes for runaway slaves was called the _____ .

a. Underground Railroad   b. Atlantic Triangle
c. Nat Turner revolt   d. northern route

3.012 Laws in the South which confirmed the belief that slaves were property and should be protected by the public were called _____ .

a. property laws   b. slave codes   c. civil codes   d. rebellion laws

3.013 The belief that the United States had a God-given right to extend its territory across the country was known as _____ .

a. regionalism   b. sectionalism   c. Manifest Destiny   d. Monroe Doctrine

3.014   A month after Abraham Lincoln's election to the presidency, the state of _____ .

a. Virginia seceded from the Union   b. Louisiana seceded from the Union
c. Mississippi seceded from the Union   d. South Carolina seceded from the Union

3.015   The president of the Confederate States of America was _____ .

a. Jefferson Davis   b. Robert E. Lee   c. Robert Anderson   d. John Breckenridge

3.016   The first capital city of the Confederation was _____ .

a. Montgomery, Alabama   b. Richmond, Virginia
c. Atlanta, Georgia   d. Memphis, Tennessee

3.017   One of the most successful plans of the Union during the Civil War was _____ .

a. the Union blockade   b. Sherman's march to the sea
c. the battle of Bull Run   d. seizure of Federal buildings

3.018   Abraham Lincoln was assassinated at the Ford Theater by _____ .

a. Andrew Johnson   b. Robert E. Lee   c. John Wilkes Booth   d. General Sherman

3.019   To help black people adjust to freedom and to help protect their civil rights, Congress established,

in 1865, the _____ .

a. Emancipation Proclamation   b. Freedman's Bureau
c. Reconstruction Act   d. Civil Rights Act

3.020   Even after the slaves were freed, they could not be employed as _____ .

a. farm laborers   b. servants   c. factory workers   d. skilled laborers

3.021   The Thirteenth Amendment to the Constitution _____ .

a. was never ratified   b. abolished slavery forever
c. gave black people voting rights   d. replaced the black codes

3.022   The Reconstruction Act of 1867 _____ .

a. divided all Confederate states into five military districts
b. gave the Confederate states money to rebuild after the war
c. freed all Civil War prisoners
d. freed all slaves

3.023   A secret organization whose members threatened and coerced black voters was _____ .

a. Ku Klux Klan   b. Knights of the White Camellia
c. White Brotherhood   d. all of the above

3.024   To keep freed black people from voting, Southern state legislatures _____ .

a. gave black people phony ballots   b. reinstated slavery
c. passed black codes   d. instituted poll taxes and literacy tests

Complete these statements (each answer, 3 points).

3.025   The publication by Thomas Paine that caused colonists to think seriously about declaring their

independence from Britain was named _____ .

3.026   The Declaration of Independence was written by _____ .

3.027   The Supreme Court case that established the principle that the Court could declare acts of

Congress unconstitutional was _____ .

3.028   The reason the United States engaged in the Louisiana Purchase was that the Port of

_____ had been closed to American traffic.

3.029   The last battle of the War of 1812 was the battle of _____ .

3.030   _____ might be defined as people living in a section of a country
interested only in how legislation affects their section.

3.031   Three sectional issues were:

_____

_____

_____

3.032   Andrew Jackson's and Thomas Jefferson's political philosophies were similar because they both

believed people should a. _____ in b. _____ .

Answer these questions (each answer, 3 points).

3.033   On June 1, 1812, President James Madison asked Congress to declare war on Great Britain.
List three reasons why.

_____

_____

_____

3.034   Two incidents that led the United States into the Spanish-American War were:

_____

_____

_____

_____

Match the following (each answer, 2 points).

3.035 _____ Alexander Hamilton

3.036 _____ Aaron Burr

3.037 _____ John Marshall

3.038 _____ Roger Williams

3.039 _____ Sojourner Truth

3.040 _____ Abraham Lincoln

3.041 _____ John Breckenridge

3.042 _____ Robert E. Lee

3.043 _____ Stonewall Jackson

3.044 _____ Theodore Roosevelt

3.045 _____ Ulysses S. Grant

3.046 _____ William T. Sherman

3.047 _____ Andrew Johnson

3.048 _____ Rutherford B. Hayes

3.049 _____ William B. McKinley

a. Confederate general who surrendered at Appomattox Court House

b. wrote a financial plan for the United States

c. United States president during the Spanish-American War

d. lost the election in the House of Representatives to Thomas Jefferson

e. won the presidency in 1876

f. chief justice of the Supreme Court

g. succeeded Abraham Lincoln as the United States president

h. founder of the Rhode Island colony

i. Northern general who destroyed everything in his way in the South

j. wrote about racial discrimination

k. Union general who met at Appomattox Court House

l. president during the Civil War

m. commander of the Rough Riders

n. the South's choice for president in 1860

o. defeated the Union army at the battle of Bull Run

94
—
117

SCORE _____

✔ **CHECK** _____ _____

Teacher   Date

4. INDUSTRIALIZATION OF THE UNITED STATES

The early 1900s brought a change that would affect this country for many years to come. That change was the Industrial Revolution, which also changed lifestyles and affected the government. It changed the entire shape of the country both literally and figuratively. Once an agrarian society with only a few textile mills, the United States in the 1900s became the manufacturer of goods not only for itself but also for other nations. Cities grew as people moved from farms to find jobs in booming factories.

Labor unions organized to protect workers from deplorable working conditions. Legislation was passed to protect both labor and management. As the nation continued to expand geographically and transportation routes were expanded to make other cities more accessible, the United States would never again be the same agricultural society of the 1800s.

Section Objectives

Review these objectives. When you have completed this section, you should be able to:

12. Explain the effect of the industrial revolution on lifestyles in the United States.

13. List the causes and the results of World War I.

14. Explain the causes and the results of the Great Depression.

15. List the provisions of Roosevelt's New Deal.

Vocabulary

Study these words to enhance your learning success in this section.

component . . . . A part or ingredient.

curtail . . . . To shorten or reduce.

defray . . . . To pay.

ironic . . . . Directly opposite from what might have been expected.

throes . . . . Pain or affliction.

THE INDUSTRIAL REVOLUTION

The United States had all the **components** for industrialization by the time the twentieth century began. The country had lived through the growing pains of colonization and the establishment of a government. It had survived, had been victorious in three wars with other nations, and had rebuilt after its own civil conflict. In addition, it was a new nation with abundant natural resources from which to manufacture goods in demand by its own people and by people of other nations.

Industrial Growth. The United States contained valuable stores of natural resources and raw materials needed for industrial growth. Coal fields as well as fertile land for crop production were abundant. Rivers and streams were a natural energy source for the powering of machinery. The United States also had a continuous supply of people for management and for production in industry. The great flow of immigrants into the country contributed to the labor supply. The United States' growing resentment of Britain also spurred its industrial growth. Britain had been slow to share its sophisticated knowledge of technology with the United States and the United States became more determined to be industrially successful.

Agricultural United States was the first sector to profit from the machine age. In 1793, Eli Whitney invented the cotton gin, which changed the slow process of separating cotton seeds from lint to a mechanized operation. The cotton gin increased cotton production substantially and opened the way for other inventions to streamline the agricultural industry. In the years after the invention of the cotton gin, Jethro Woods invented the iron plow, James Oliver invented the chilled plow, and Cyrus McCormick invented the reaping machine. Elias Howe invented the sewing machine, which speeded up the slow process of making clothing by hand and decreased the price of clothing.

Industrial growth demanded the expansion of transportation systems in the country. In the early 1800s work was begun on the first national road. The road started in Cumberland, Maryland and ended in Wheeling, Virginia, now West Virginia. It was used by farmers, cattlemen, traders, and manufacturers to distribute goods and materials to other parts of the small country. The Cumberland Road inspired the states to build roads of their own. Many were toll roads and the money collected was used to **defray** the cost of construction.

Road travel was slow; consequently, industry often shipped its goods by water. Canals were built to increase water-travel efficiency. One such canal was the Erie Canal that connected Lake Erie with the Hudson River in New York. This enabled ships that reached the Hudson to travel through New York and into the Atlantic Ocean.

The age of water travel inspired Robert Fulton's development of the steamboat in 1807. His steamship, the Clermont, traveled successfully in a three-hundred-mile trip on the Hudson from New York City to Albany. Within a few years, steamboats were traveling regularly down the country's major rivers.

In some areas of the country, rivers and streams were not plentiful and water travel was impossible. These areas, nevertheless, needed improved transportation. The steam engine was modified to land travel in the form of steam locomotives, such as Peter Cooper's *Tom Thumb*. Soon track was laid and the train became a viable means of travel for people and for goods. By 1860, over thirty thousand miles of railroad track had been laid across the country.

Inventions to serve transportation were not the only inventions of the time. Developments in communication were equally important to an industrially growing country. In 1844, Samuel F. B. Morse showed how messages could be sent over electric telegraph wires. His invention resulted in the installation of fifty thousand miles of telegraph lines reaching from the East Coast to California.

The wars of the 1800s also spurred the development of the inventions of war. The production of new weapons, ammunition, and other military equipment kept factories busy.

Complete these statements.

4.1   The vocabulary word _____ means *to pay*.

4.2   The vocabulary word _____ means *a part* or *ingredient*.

Complete this activity.

4.3   Write a paragraph in which you discuss the conditions that led to the industrial development of the United States.

_____

_____

_____

_____

_____

_____

Economic Expansion. The invention of labor-saving devices put more and more goods into the hands of people at a lower price. For goods to be manufactured at low prices, a factory system needed to be developed.

Eli Whitney, developer of the cotton gin, worked on a system of factory production. He had been a gun maker in Britain and while there he developed a system of standardized parts for gun making. Parts for his guns could be used interchangeably and if a part broke down or wore out, it could be quickly replaced by another part. Other manufacturers quickly picked up Whitney's system.

Henry Ford's use of the assembly line in the automotive industry advanced manufacturing tremendously. Ford used Whitney's system of standardized parts on a moving assembly line. As a result the Model T Ford, which was mass produced in 1901, became the most successful passenger car of the time.

Power sources were discovered in the late 1800s. Oil was discovered in 1859 by Edwin L. Drake near Titusville, Pennsylvania. At first oil was used only to make machine parts run smoothly and to light kerosene lamps. Later it was used instead of coal to produce steam. Gasoline was eventually used in internal combustion engines.

Another new power source of the time was electricity. Thomas A. Edison succeeded in developing a luminous lamp in October, 1879. Electricity became a versatile power source that supplied light, operated communication systems, and supplied power for all kinds of manufacturing.

The invention of the internal combustion engine spurred the invention of the horseless carriage in the 1890s. Designers such as Charles and Frank Duryea, Henry Ford and Henry Olds created many successful automobiles. Ford's use of assembly-line methods made automobiles available to people at lower costs and added mobility to people's lives. Trucks provided another means of transporting goods across the country.

Transportation was further advanced with the invention of the airplane. Wilbur and Orville Wright piloted the first successful aircraft on December 17, 1903. The Wright brothers later sold an airplane to the army, introducing air power to the military. Further work and improvements developed the commercial airlines, the forerunners of the jet age.

The growth of factories, transportation, communication, and the advent of mass production between 1860 and 1894 caused the United States to advance from fourth to first place among industrial nations in the world. During that time industry rapidly replaced agriculture in the economy. The major industries in the early 1900s were food products, textiles, iron and steel, and lumber.

Other inventors who had learned to send sound over wires inspired Alexander Graham Bell to invent the telephone. On March 10, 1876, he sent his first telephone message. The invention was refined by the American Bell Telephone Company and by 1902 more than one million telephones were in the United States.

Match the following.

4.4 _____ Eli Whitney

4.5 _____ Henry Ford

4.6 _____ Edwin L. Drake

4.7 _____ Henry Olds

4.8 _____ Wilbur and Orville Wright

4.9 _____ Thomas A. Edison

4.10 _____ Alexander Graham Bell

a. invented the telephone

b. invented the electric light

c. responsible for factory assembly lines

d. responsible for standardized parts

e. discovered oil

f. designer of non-Ford automobile

g. invented the airplane

Industrial Effects on Life. With industrialization, life in the United States changed markedly. Small companies could neither survive the competition of large industries nor afford the sophisticated equipment needed to produce low cost goods. Small companies needed capital for machinery and needed to remain competitive. These needs led to the development of the United States' corporation system. To form a corporation, several companies and business people pooled their capital and formed one organization. The people submitted a formal request to the government to establish the corporation. People would then invest their money in the corporation in exchange for stock certificates. The stockholders became part owners and elected boards of directors who appointed company officials to run the corporation and to determine its policies. Stockholders shared in the profits.

In some cases strong corporations expanded to such an extent that they became monopolies of their product. By 1905, eleven percent of businesses controlled more that eighty percent of the capital, employed seventy-two percent of the laborers, and produced seventy-nine percent of the manufactured goods. Many individuals became wealthy and influential through industrial careers.

During his presidency, Theodore Roosevelt, successfully changed some past monopolistic practices. Roosevelt strictly enforced earlier laws against any corporations that were selling low quality goods at inflated prices because they lacked competition. He also made the public aware of monopolistic industrial practices and gained more cooperation from business in treating the consumer fairly.

Other measures to control large corporations included the Clayton Anti-Trust Act of 1914 and the setting up of the Federal Trade Commission. The Clayton Act outlawed big business methods of discouraging competition. The Federal Trade Commission was responsible for seeing that antitrust laws were enforced and that small businesses were protected. The power of big businesses and monopolies was kept in better check.

Industrialization attracted people in search of large factory salaries, city excitement, or an opportunity to leave rural areas. Many who moved to the cities were unable to find homes they could afford on small salaries and resorted to the dirty, cramped quarters of the city tenements. City services at that time were practically nonexistent. No public transportation was available and little recreation space was set aside for the children. Freedom was limited. The factory worker was virtually at the mercy of the factory owner for his livelihood. Even with these conditions more and more people flocked to the city. Urbanization was becoming a reality and city populations increased.

Although industrialization relieved people of heavy, manual labor, it also robbed people of important values. People no longer had independence, creativity, or a sense of self worth. People lost these values because of the class structure within the factories. Factory workers either directed the work or did the work. Those who directed the work were paid a salary; those who did the work were paid daily or weekly wages for the work performed. They helped the owners become wealthy, but they did not share in the wealth and comforts they helped produce. The factory system was highly impersonal and working conditions were often poor. Factories were poorly ventilated and were usually hot and muggy in the summer and cold and damp in the winter. No accident insurance or compensation for injury was provided; therefore, victims of industrial accidents had little choice but to terminate their jobs if they were injured. A normal work day was twelve to sixteen hours a day and wages were about six dollars a week. Because wages were so low, many women and children had to work to keep food on the table.

Women and children were treated poorly in factories, but they were preferred by factory owners because they would accept less pay than men. Children were sometimes beaten if they fell asleep on the job and they were forced to pull heavy carts in the coal mines in places too low for adults to work. Factory work was also uncertain. When factories were overstocked, workers were laid off, their wages were reduced or production was reduced. No unemployment insurance was provided and such workers were forced to beg in the streets or to look for work in another factory. Such conditions led eventually to unionism.

Unionism. Factory workers' problems developed because of large corporations. When companies were small and were run by partnerships and individual owners, the owners were aware of the problems and concerns of their workers. Owners were personally acquainted with the workers. With the rise of large corporations, personal relationships between owner and workers vanished. Dissatisfied workers could easily be replaced.

Workers realized they needed to band together to change the conditions in factories. At first, workers disagreed on goals and how they should be achieved; however, the labor union movement finally began with the organization of the National

| Poor factory conditions and worker abuse led to unions that protected workers' treatment.

Labor Union (NLU) in 1866. Goals of the NLU were to curb inflation and to reduce working hours to an eight-hour workday. When the NLU attempted to become involved in politics in 1872, it collapsed.

Big business tried battling unionism by blacklisting union leaders from jobs, firing them, and legally prosecuting them. As a result, much labor union activity was carried on in secret.

In 1868, the Knights of Labor was organized and was headed by Uriah S. Stephens. The union admitted all workers and tried to educate public opinion to the union's goals. As the union grew, it used strikes as a method of fighting blacklisting and prosecution of union leaders. The most publicized strikes of that time were the Great Railroad Strikes of 1877. Violence erupted and soldiers were mobilized to restore order although many workers were injured and millions of dollars of property damage resulted.

In 1886, the American Federation of Labor (AFL) was formed to charter and to strengthen national unions. Initially the AFL believed that labor was entitled to share in the profits of big business. Samuel Gompers was the first AFL president.

Unions were valuable in promoting collective bargaining between labor and employers and they brought about many reforms in working conditions and worker benefits through government legislation. The worker had finally received a voice in making their needs known and remedied.

Complete these statements.

4.11 To gain capital for expanding their factories, small companies formed _____ by pooling their capital.

4.12 Part owners in companies who elected the boards of directors were _____ .

4.13 Large corporations that controlled the markets of certain products and drove out competition from other companies are called _____ .

4.14 Two measures passed to control large corporations are the _____ and the _____ .

4.15 Workers banded together into _____ to change conditions in the factories.

4.16 The first organized union in the United States was the _____ .

4.17 The organization developed to strengthen and charter national unions was the

_____ .

WORLD WAR I

During the early 1900s, friction between countries grew and was spurred on by the growing feelings of nationalism among the people toward their country. Imperialism also increased as countries began to expand. Governments looked beyond their borders for areas they could conquer that would make their countries stronger and wealthier. Increased nationalism and interests in imperialism led to increased support of the military. Armies and navies were developed to give countries international advantage.

The event that led to World War I was the assassination of Austrian Archduke Francis Ferdinand and his wife by a member of a Serbian secret society on June 18, 1914. Austria, assured of Germany's support, declared war on Serbia. Russia sided with Serbia and Germany declared war on Russia and its ally France. Although Belgium was neutral, Germany marched across that country anyway. That action caused an international uproar and caused Great Britain to join forces with France and Russia. Later, Italy joined the war in 1915 as an ally of Russia, France, and Britain.

During the war, Germany had little trouble overcoming Russia, but French resistance was much stronger than expected. The Allies, consisting of Great Britain, France, Serbia (Yugoslavia), Belgium, Japan, and Montenegro (Yugoslavia), were defeated in their efforts to aid Russia. By 1916, the war had reached a stalemate.

The United States had remained neutral from the beginning but eventually had to make a choice and most Americans supported the Allied powers. When Germany began sinking United States supply ships heading for Britain and France, the United States also declared war on Germany and entered the war.

The United States Navy was well prepared for war; but the army was small, ill-equipped, and poorly trained. The problems were alleviated by the Selective Service Act that drafted eligible men between the ages of twenty-one and thirty.

| World War I German battleship

Although the Germans tried to end the war before the Allies were reinforced by United States troops, they were unsuccessful. When American troops arrived in 1917, the Allies became more powerful and more successful. Victories included the battle at Cantigny, the Argonne Forest, and Chateau Thierry. An armistice was signed on November 11, 1918.

After the four-year war, people were eager for peace. President Woodrow Wilson, even before the war ended, presented to Congress his Fourteen Points Peace Plan. He advocated no secret international agreements, freedom of the seas outside territorial waters, the removal of economic barriers, the establishment of equal trade conditions among nations, and a reduction of national armaments. Wilson also advocated impartial adjustments of colonial claims, evacuation of all German troops from Russia and the opportunity for Russia to determine its own political development. He further recommended the evacuation and restoration of Belgium, the restoration of France, and the return of Alsace-Lorraine to France. In addition, Wilson advocated a readjustment of the Italian frontier, limited self government for Austria-Hungary, and the reconstruction and independence of Balkan states with access of the sea.

Finally, he proposed self-determination for Turkey, independence for Poland, and the formation of a general association of nations.

Wilson's ideas of a just peace were not echoed by all. Some countries proposed peace with vengeance. The fate of the plan would be made in Paris in January, 1919, when the thirty Allied countries met. Representatives of the five great powers were present: Britain, France, Italy, the United States, and Japan.

Wilson believed a League of Nations was vital to peace and he spent much time at the peace conference on the formation of the organization. His League of Nations would regulate international relations, would limit armaments, and would settle disagreements between nations in a peaceful way. His other ideas were not accepted, but he signed the Treaty of Versailles. The German government grudgingly approved the treaty in May, 1919. His ideas for a League of Nations were accepted unanimously by the Allied representatives. **Ironically**, the United States later voted against joining the League of Nations, and because of that move, other nations lost confidence in the League.

Match these vocabulary words with their proper definitions.

4.18 _____ curtail

4.19 _____ ironic

4.20 _____ throes

a. pain or affliction

b. to shorten or reduce

c. directly opposite from what might have been expected

Complete this activity.

4.21 Write a paragraph in which you explain how nationalism contributed to the United States entering World War I.

_____

_____

_____

_____

_____

_____

_____

GREAT DEPRESSION

The period preceding the Great Depression was generally one of prosperity and achievement for the United States. Two controversies, however, had occupied the minds of people in the early 1920s: the scandals of the Harding Administration and prohibition. Harding's administration was accused of receiving money for pardons and illicit activities such as liquor distribution during prohibition. The Teapot Dome Scandal also occurred during his administration.

The Teapot Dome Scandal involved policies on the leasing of oil reserves. Control of these oil reserves was transferred from the Navy Department to the Department of the Interior. The Department of the Interior was headed by Albert B. Fall, one of President Harding's cabinet members and closest friends. Secretary Fall leased the Teapot Dome reserve illegally without public bids. The persons to whom the reserves were leased received large profits as a result of the lease. Later, Secretary Fall was convicted of receiving a bribe, was fined, and was sent to jail.

Calvin Coolidge became President when Harding died. President Coolidge was not a strong leader, but he was honest and moral. His popularity remained strong throughout his term in office. His early disagreements with farmers over farm relief and higher prices for farm products were erased because farmers were experiencing prosperity. When Coolidge completed his term of office, the people were confident and optimistic about the future.

Hoover Administration. Herbert Hoover became President in 1929 under favorable economic conditions. The nation had enjoyed one of the most prosperous periods in its history between 1923 and 1929. Goods were being produced at a rapid rate. Although some people were poor, the majority of the people experienced prosperity and achievement. Construction flourished as World War I veterans returned to build new homes. Jobs were plentiful, wages were rising, and unionization seemed strongly entrenched.

Economic Conditions. Even with favorable economic conditions in the twenties, major defects soon appeared. Some large industries were not as successful as they appeared. Furthermore, many farmers were producing more than they could sell and, as food prices fell, farmers realized lower profits.

Competition from foreign countries complicated matters. The United States foreign trade program was also unhealthy. Foreign exports exceeded imports, but loans from foreign countries were accepted as payment for goods purchased from the United States.

A problem with credit was apparent. People who could not afford products began buying them on credit. However, without available credit, customer purchases were **curtailed**; and products were not sold. A decrease in customer buying led to unemployment. More and more economists were aware that the prosperity was artificial. In addition, stock prices increased with speculative buying rather than with cash.

On October 29, 1929, the stock market collapsed as frantic sellers offered 16,410,000 shares to sell for practically nothing. Hundreds of thousands of stockholders went bankrupt. The Great Depression had begun.

The depression affected the American people in different ways. Some wealthy people became paupers overnight; others had enough wealth to absorb the loss. Many workers were laid off, but some business people remained on their jobs. Those people without jobs sought unemployment relief and free meals at public kitchens. Some people lost their homes when banks to whom they owed money foreclosed on loans.

The government initially offered little relief. Congress did pass a bill that authorized the distribution of wheat and cotton to the people. Money was also appropriated for rediscount banks that gave credit to banks and to financial institutions. Congress also provided for the Home Loan Bank System to help homeowners who were about to lose their homes.

Complete this activity.

4.22 List the events that led to the Great Depression.

a. _____

b. _____

c. _____

d. _____

e. _____

f. _____

g. _____

Match the following.

4.23	_____	Albert B. Fall	**a.** many scandals during his administration
4.24	_____	Warren G. Harding	**b.** became president after Harding's death
4.25	_____	Calvin Coolidge	**c.** president during the Great Depression
4.26	_____	Herbert Hoover	**d.** Teapot Dome Scandal

NEW DEAL

The New Deal, a program promised by Franklin D. Roosevelt during his campaign for the presidency, set policies that promised to cure the injustices within the business and the financial communities. It also promised relief to labor and to agricultural groups, and it was welcomed by a nation that was still in the **throes** of a depression. Roosevelt was elected President in 1932 and his New Deal was implemented.

President Roosevelt planned to distribute the nation's abundance to those most in need. His belief was that if the private sector would not solve the nation's economic problems, then the government would solve them. In his inaugural address Roosevelt called for strict control of banking and credit, a work project to employ the jobless, and a Good Neighbor Policy in world affairs as a way to lift the country from the depression.

Roosevelt's plan was to build from the bottom up with the foundation being the hard working common person. He also promised a tariff reduction to encourage international trade. To implement the

New Deal, Roosevelt chose competent, loyal cabinet members who believed in the ability of the president to get the job done.

Roosevelt's plan was based upon immediate action. He theorized that any legislation put through Congress was better than standing still. One of the first bills introduced to Congress was the Emergency Banking Act, a bill that prevented panic withdrawals of funds from banks by the public. The act also called for banks to close, to be evaluated by the government, and to reopen only if they were fiscally sound. The act helped the people regain confidence in the banking system and money was returned to most banks.

To reduce unemployment, Congress established the Civilian Conservation Corps (CCC), that gave jobs to young men. They received thirty dollars a month for maintaining parks and working on building projects. With the Federal Emergency Relief Act, 500 million dollars was appropriated to help individual states obtain unemployment relief. The Agricultural

Adjustment Act gave farmers higher prices for less production, and they were paid to farm only certain amounts of acreage. In addition, the National Industrial Recovery Act attempted to get private companies to establish business codes together to prevent bad competition practices common before the depression. The law was eventually declared unconstitutional; but it did pave the way for minimum and maximum wage standards, for laws to correct the abuses of child labor, and for collective bargaining laws for workers. The Social Security Act answered the demands for the distribution of wealth and support for the aged. The act provided for old-age pension, old-age insurance, unemployment insurance, and other public health programs. Roosevelt was also influential in the establishment of the Tennessee Valley Authority. Dams were built on the Tennessee River to provide flood control and electrical energy.

Roosevelt was overwhelmingly re-elected in 1936. His major problem was to protect his New Deal from opposition in the Supreme Court. The Court hindered the plan by declaring certain measures unconstitutional. Roosevelt's New Deal also helped minority groups in the country, reducing unemployment for black people, tenant farmers, and migrant workers.

By the end of the 1930s the United States was slowly recovering from the depression. Millions were back at work, economic problems were gradually being solved, and the people could see that living conditions had improved.

Complete this activity.

4.27 The New Deal was a program promised by _____ during his campaign for the presidency.

Put a check beside the correct answer(s).

4.28 The New Deal set two policies that promised

_____ to allow the private sector to solve the nation's economic problems.

_____ to cure the injustices within the business and the financial communities.

_____ to increase trade through tariff protection.

_____ to give relief to labor and to agricultural groups.

4.29 Select the four bills sent to Congress implementing Roosevelt's New Deal.

_____ Federal Emergency Relief Act

_____ Social Security Act

_____ National Agricultural Recovery Act

_____ Emergency Banking Act

_____ Agricultural Adjustment Act

_____ Tennessee Valley Authority Act

_____ Civilian Conservation Act

↺ **Review the material in this section in preparation for the Self Test.** The Self Test will check your mastery of this particular section as well as your knowledge of the previous sections.

SELF TEST 4

Answer *true* **or** *false* (each answer, 1 point).

4.01 _____ Before the Industrial Revolution, the United States became resentful of Britain for not sharing its technology with the United States.

4.02 _____ The first national road began in New York and ended in Wheeling, West Virginia.

4.03 _____ The Erie Canal connected Lake Erie with the Hudson River.

4.04 _____ Major industries in the early 1900s were food products, textiles, iron and steel, and lumber.

4.05 _____ The United States corporation system was an outgrowth of the New Deal.

4.06 _____ Strong corporations were prevented in the early 1900s from becoming monopolies.

4.07 _____ The Federal Trade Commission was responsible for protecting large corporations.

4.08 _____ During his administration, James Madison prevented the National Bank from going out of business.

4.09 _____ The Missouri Compromise of 1820 allowed Maine to be admitted to the Union as a free state.

4.010 _____ Industries in the late 1800s did not provide accident insurance for workers.

Match the following (each answer, 2 points).

4.011 _____ Eli Whitney

4.012 _____ Cyrus McCormick

4.013 _____ Elias Howe

4.014 _____ Samuel F. B. Morse

4.015 _____ Henry Ford

4.016 _____ Edwin L. Drake

4.017 _____ Wilbur and Orville Wright

4.018 _____ Alexander Graham Bell

4.019 _____ Uriah S. Stephens

4.020 _____ Samuel Gompers

4.021 _____ Archduke Francis Ferdinand

4.022 _____ Woodrow Wilson

4.023 _____ Franklin Roosevelt

4.024 _____ Warren G. Harding

4.025 _____ Herbert Hoover

a. the telephone

b. the Great Depression

c. standardized parts

d. Teapot Dome scandal

e. the reaping machine

f. New Deal

g. sewing machine

h. League of Nations

i. telegraph

j. death that began World War I

k. factory assembly lines

l. American Federation of Labor

m. oil

n. Knights of Labor

o. airplane

Write the letter of the correct answer on each line (each answer, 2 points).

4.026 The New Deal was designed to distribute the nation's abundance to _____ .

   a. private industry   b. foreign countries   c. those most in need   d. minorities only

4.027 Roosevelt considered the foundation of the New Deal to be _____ .

   a. government   b. common hard-working people
   c. executives of large banks   d. the Congress

4.028 In world affairs Roosevelt advocated a _____ .

   a. policy of isolationism   b. policy of extreme nationalism
   c. Good Neighbor Policy   d. policy of expansion

4.029 One provision of the Emergency Banking Bill was _____ .

   a. prevention of panic withdrawals   b. the opening of all banks
   c. an increase of bank reserves   d. an establishment of state banks immediately

4.030 The Act that provided for old-age pensions and unemployment insurance was _____ .

   a. the Agricultural Adjustment Act   b. the Social Security Act
   c. the National Industrial Recovery Act   d. the Federal Emergency Relief Act

4.031 Roosevelt received opposition to the New Deal from _____ .

   a. his Cabinet   b. the Congress
   c. the majority of people   d. the Supreme Court

4.032 The invention of the sewing machine resulted in _____ .

   a. more fashionable garments   b. lower-priced clothing
   c. better tailoring of clothing   d. fewer jobs for people

4.033 The United States' status of first place among industrial nations was a result, in part, of _____ .

   a. an industrial slowdown in Europe   b. its many resources
   c. the growth of the agricultural industry   d. the War of 1812

4.034 To gain more capital for industrial expansion, small companies _____ .

   a. formed corporations   b. borrowed money from banks
   c. produced more goods   d. formed partnerships

4.035 Stockholders of a company _____ .

   a. invest their money in the company   b. elect the board of directors
   c. share in the company profits   d. all of the above

4.036 Strong corporations that expand to the extent that they greatly reduce competition are called

   _____ .

   a. partnerships   b. big business   c. monopolies   d. stock companies

4.037 People moved into cities during the Industrial Revolution because _____ .

a. they wanted high factory wages
b. they had lost their homes during the Depression
c. they were attracted by the abundance of city services
d. they were recruited by city factory owners

4.038 When unions were first organized, union leaders _____ .

a. were paid larger salaries than nonunion workers
b. promoted strikes among factory workers
c. were blacklisted by factory owners
d. were seriously listened to by factory owners

4.039 A government's desire to conquer areas beyond its border for wealth and strength is an example

of _____ .

a. nationalism   b. imperialism   c. sectionalism   d. isolationism

4.040 The event that led to United States involvement in World War I was _____ .

a. the assassination of Archduke Ferdinand
b. Britain's declaration of war
c. the bombing of the *Maine*
d. Germany's sinking of United States' supply ships

4.041 The New Deal was a set of policies that promised to _____ .

a. keep the United States out of war
b. expand the United States' sphere of influence in the world
c. cure injustices within the business and financial communities
d. expand industrialization in the United States

Complete these statements (each answer, 3 points).

4.042 Roosevelt's New Deal focused on a. _____ methods instead of

b. _____ methods for relieving the nation of the depression.

4.043 Roosevelt's Emergency Banking Act prevented panic _____ and banks
were closed for government evaluation of solvency.

4.044 The invention that increased river transportation was Fulton's _____ .

4.045 What three things made the United States a logical country for industrialization?

a. _____

b. _____

c. _____

74/93 **SCORE** _____   ✓ **CHECK** _____ _____
                                                    Teacher   Date

5. THE UNITED STATES: ROOSEVELT TO TRUMP

The United States was not the only country to suffer from the depression of the 1930s. The effects of the economic collapse were worldwide with many European people suffering unemployment, hunger, and loss of possessions. To stimulate the economy and to end unemployment, many nations concentrated on the production of war materials. Military buildup in larger nations caused smaller nations to become tense and feel threatened by the thrust of great military powers. The tension and hostilities eventually resulted in World War II.

Other conflicts surfaced between 1950 and 1979. The Korean conflict and the Vietnam War involved the United States further in world problems. U.S. Presidents Kennedy, Johnson, Nixon, and Ford were influential in bringing these conflicts to an end. They also proposed numerous domestic plans to improve conditions at home. In this section you will review United States history from 1940 through the Trump Administration. You will learn about the conflicts through which modern contemporary people have lived.

Section Objectives

Review these objectives. When you have completed this section, you should be able to:

16. Identify the causes and results of World War II.

17. Identify the causes and results of the wars in Korea and Vietnam.

18. List major contributions of the administrations of Presidents Kennedy, Johnson, Nixon, and Ford.

19. Explain the reasons for President Nixon's resignation.

20. List the major contributions of the administrations of Presidents Carter, Reagan, George H. W. Bush, Clinton, George W. Bush, Obama, and Trump.

21. Explain the major events shortly before and after the New Millennium.

Vocabulary

Study these words to enhance your learning success in this section.

surveillance . . . . To observe closely; to be watchful.

implicate . . . . To be involved in some matter.

predicate . . . . To affirm, assert, or to declare.

WORLD WAR II

World War II affected more people's lives than any other war in the history of the United States. World War II brought atomic warfare and other significant changes in war tactics. War tactics, such as bombings, ballistic missiles, warships, and airplanes that dropped paratroopers into enemy jungles, were the rule. The war cost $3.5 trillion and killed 10 million Allied troops and 6 million Axis troops. More than fifty countries were involved in the global war.

Significant Causes. The effects of the Depression in Europe were, in part, responsible for World War II. In desperation, the people of Germany allowed themselves to be led by a ruthless leader named Adolf Hitler who promoted fascism. Hitler came to power through the appointment as chancellor by President Paul Von Hindenburg. Many Germans hoped the appointment would both strengthen and unite the country.

Hitler reduced unemployment in Germany by building up the military and by establishing branches of the National Socialist Party's (Nazi) youth movement. The military buildup was in direct violation of the Versailles Treaty that prohibited military growth. At the same time, Benito Mussolini, premier and dictator of Italy, was limiting unemployment by building up a large military. The Japanese were also having economic problems; and to solve them, they were taking control of various islands for their natural resources.

President von Hindenburg died in 1934 and the world saw Adolf Hitler's obsession with personal power. Hitler disposed of his opponents and declared himself dictator. He then began to break restrictions placed on Germany by the Versailles Treaty. Other nations were careful to avoid conflict with Germany. As the rest of the world stood by in 1938, the Nazis seized Austria; in 1939, they invaded Czechoslovakia. At last the European nations were forced to act. When Hitler invaded Poland in

| *USS Arizona* on fire in Pearl Harbor attack

September, 1939, Britain immediately declared war on Germany. France soon joined Britain, but Italy later sided with Hitler. The last nation to join Italy and Germany was Japan. That alliance then became known as the Axis Powers.

Japanese-American relations had been strained for some time because of their competition in trade. Japanese diplomats met in Washington with United States' officials supposedly to settle trade disagreements. At the same time, Japanese pilots were preparing to secretly bomb Pearl Harbor in the Hawaiian Islands. On December 7, 1941, United States' sailors awoke to a torrent of bombs and bullets. Tragically, over three thousand sailors and soldiers were killed as a result of the sneak attack.

The United States could no longer avoid war and the United States' Congress, on December 8, 1941, declared war on Japan. Because the navy had been severely crippled by the Pearl Harbor attack, the United States entered the war at a disadvantage.

Complete these activities.

5.1   The vocabulary word meaning *to observe closely* or *to be watchful* is

_____ .

5.2   In what four ways did Hitler break the Versailles Treaty?

_____

_____

_____

_____

Answer *true* **or** *false.*

5.3   _____   Germany's attack on Pearl Harbor was one event that led to the United States' involvement in World War II.

5.4   _____   Hitler's attacks of smaller countries and military buildups as a result of economic depression led to Europe's involvement in World War II.

Major Battles. The United States entered the war two years after it had begun, and those two years had been successful for the Germans. German military officers were well disciplined and equipment was plentiful. Activity in the war slowed somewhat after Hitler's initial attacks. Then Germany invaded Scandinavia, Holland, Belgium, and Luxembourg. The British were no match for the powerful military machine and Germany won these conquests also.

By this time, Italy had joined Germany and France had been conquered. As a result Britain had to face Germany alone. The United States supplied the British with as much support as possible without actually fighting. In June, 1942, Germany invaded the Soviet Union, but the Soviets were able to resist and to counterattack driving the Germans back.

After the United States declared war on Japan, it agreed to send troops to Europe. Led by General Dwight D. Eisenhower, the troops landed in North Africa. With the help of the British, United States' troops were able to drive the Germans out. This defeat and the fight with Russia seriously weakened the German forces.

Italy became another battleground for fierce fighting between the Allied and Axis powers. When the Italian army was driven out of the war, divisions of German troops rushed in to hold the Italian Peninsula.

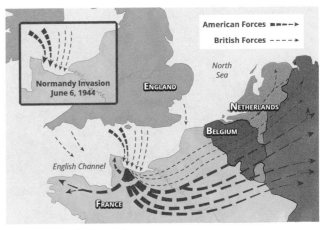

| Normandy Invasion

The next plan of the Allies was the invasion of German-occupied France. Forces were gathered in Great Britain to await the perfect time for the attack. The invasion was well planned. Fake paratroopers and supplies were dropped in another location to confuse the German army. On June 6, the invasion occurred as hundreds of planes began bombing France. The Germans resisted but the invasion of Normandy ultimately defeated the German army.

From Normandy the Allies drove across France and into Germany itself. Meanwhile, the Russians closed in on the Germans from the east. Nazi generals fled the country and Hitler committed suicide. The war in Europe finally ended on May 8, 1945.

On the Pacific front immediately after the attack on Pearl Harbor in December, 1941, the United States established a defensive policy. The Japanese, however, began invading numerous Pacific islands and built up strongholds hoping to prevent the Allies from reaching Japan. General Douglas MacArthur led the United States' military in the Pacific campaign.

The United States debated hard and long about alternatives to terminate the war and decided to bomb Tokyo. Lieutenant Colonel James H. Doolittle was the leader of the air attack on Tokyo. The attack was a complete surprise to the Japanese. Because their **surveillance** was far enough into the Pacific Ocean, they thought no bomber could possibly take off without being detected. The successful air attack occurred on April 18, 1942 and it put the United States in a more aggressive role in the war.

The Pacific campaign was largely naval with marines doing most of the land fighting. Following successful naval and air battles, the United States planned a series of island hopping conquests to drive the Japanese gradually back toward their homeland. The struggle was hard and bitter, but the United States met it with success.

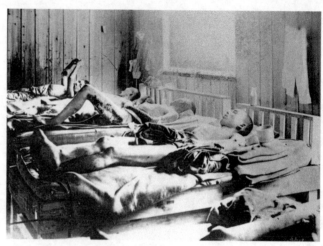

| Survivors of the atomic bomb on Hiroshima

Plans continued for the invasion of Japan. President Harry S. Truman decided that atomic bombs would be dropped on the cities of Hiroshima and Nagasaki. The dropping of these awesome and devastating bombs brought about the surrender of the Japanese on August 10, 1945.

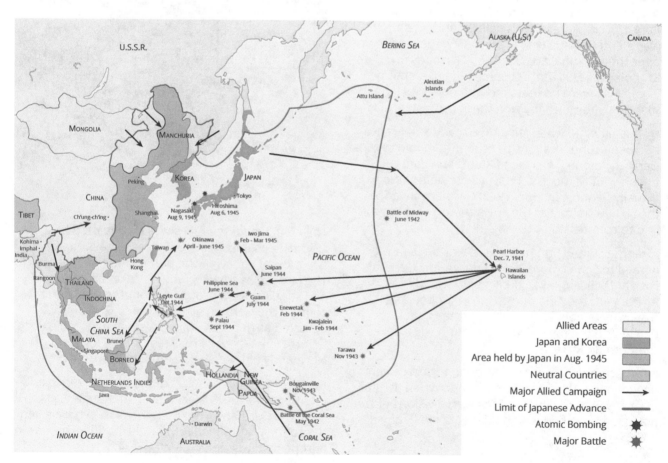

Answer *true* **or** *false*.

5.5 _____ The United States entered the war immediately after it began.

5.6 _____ The Russians offered strong resistance to the German attack.

5.7 _____ After the United States declared war on Japan, it agreed to send troops to Europe also.

5.8 _____ The bombing of Tokyo brought the war in the Pacific to an end.

5.9 _____ The Pacific campaign was largely conducted by the navy and the marines.

Match the following.

5.10 _____ Dwight D. Eisenhower

5.11 _____ Adolf Hitler

5.12 _____ James H. Doolittle

5.13 _____ Harry S. Truman

5.14 _____ Douglas MacArthur

a. led military in the Pacific

b. landed troops on North Africa

c. President who decided to drop the A-bomb on Hiroshima

d. dictator of Germany

e. leader of Tokyo bombing

KOREAN CONFLICT

The term *cold war* differs from a hot war. A hot war involves actual combat, such as World War II. Cold War refers to hostilities and differences that occur between nations that have not resulted in physical battles.

Cold War issues were a prelude to the Korean conflict. The United Nations, an assembly that included representatives from almost every nation, was established at the end of World War II. Its function was to deal with problems that might arise between nations and hopefully to prevent a hot war.

Communism soon became an issue, particularly, in the Far East. In June, 1950, North Korean Communists attacked South Korea. The United States had hoped not to become involved, but that hope was not realized. The North Korean army pushed the South Korean army to the southernmost part of the peninsula. Syngman Rhee of South Korea pleaded with the United Nations and the United States for help. President Truman immediately supplied air and sea support. This aid was not sufficient and the United States was forced to provide ground forces under the direction of General Douglas MacArthur.

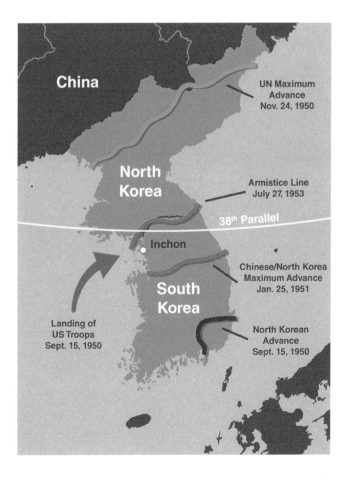

On September 15, 1950, the United States Army made a surprise attack and cut the North Korean forces in half. By autumn of 1950, the efforts of the United States and the South Korean soldiers had driven the Communists to the border between North Korea and Manchuria.

The surprise entrance of Chinese "volunteers" shortly after that caused the United States and South Korea to be pushed back. Even with the entrance of the United States' Marines, by January, 1951, the United States, South Korea, and other United Nations' groups had been forced to retreat.

In October, 1951, peace negotiations began in Panmunjom, Korea, but fighting continued for two more years. In July, 1953, a permanent armistice was signed. The United Nations referred to their intervention in Korea as a police action, a major test for the United Nations.

Write the letter of the correct answer on the line.

5.15   How did Cold War issues contribute to the Korean War? _____

    a. The conflict over communism eventually led to the invasion of North and South Korea.
    b. The conflict over industrialization eventually led to the invasion of North Korea.
    c. The conflict over communism eventually led to the invasion of South Korea.

Answer *true* **or** *false*.

5.16   _____   The United States became involved in the Korean conflict because Syngman Rhee pleaded for help.

5.17   _____   The United Nations assisted in the Korean conflict by sending troops into China.

VIETNAM WAR

The Vietnam conflict, like the Korean conflict, had occurred when Cold War issues became hot war conflicts. In the case of Vietnam, the Cold War issue was again communism and the efforts of communists to influence neutral nations to adopt their political philosophies.

Prewar. The expansion of communism in Asia became a real threat to non-communist nations. To deal with that threat, Great Britain, Australia, France, Pakistan, New Zealand, Thailand, the Philippines, and the United States formed the Southeast Asia Treaty Organization (SEATO). SEATO and NATO (North Atlantic Treaty Organization) were effective against communism in Europe and Asia, but the Soviet Union continued to infiltrate the Middle East, Latin America, and Africa. The United States offered assistance of military aid, advice, and overall availability.

War. In the early 1960s, unresolved hostilities in the Southeast Asian countries, including Vietnam, erupted into civil war. The Communist guerrilla forces in North Vietnam led by Ho Chi Minh moved closer to a takeover of the South Vietnamese government. United States President John F. Kennedy was determined to help the South Vietnamese. He offered military aid and sent military advisors to help train the South Vietnamese troops. Even after the aid, the South Vietnamese situation seemed to deteriorate and the war became more intense.

When Lyndon Johnson became president following the assassination of President John Kennedy, he vowed to take strong action in Southeast Asia to keep communism from advancing into the Pacific area. The United States then found itself becoming more involved in the war and gradually assumed a more active role in the combat. By 1964 twenty thousand United States troops were in Vietnam.

In August, 1964, President Johnson asked Congress to pass a resolution concerning the Southeast Asia conflict. Congress accepted the Gulf of Tonkin resolution. The resolution gave the President authority to retaliate militarily for the attack on United States ships in the Gulf of Tonkin and for other similar incidents. The resolution marked the beginning of the arms and troops buildup.

The war was intensified when several United States advisors were killed. In retaliation, Johnson authorized the bombing of a North Vietnamese port, thinking that action would bring a quick end to the war. Instead, the fighting became even more intense. As soon as United States' troops left a conquered area, the Viet Cong returned. Some villages were captured and recaptured many times.

As the war continued, many people in the United States became dissatisfied and urged an end to the country's involvement in Vietnam. The unpopular war received little moral support and even the United States' servicemen in Vietnam were not considered heroes. United States' victories received little credit. The people at home appeared to be more concerned with Johnson's Great Society program.

By 1968, more and more people were questioning the United States' involvement in Vietnam. Richard M. Nixon, who was elected president after Johnson chose not to run for the presidency, began a plan of Vietnamization. The first step of the plan was the withdrawal of 25,000 servicemen from Vietnam. The plan was that these troops would be replaced by South Vietnamese troops. As peace talks were being held in Paris, Nixon continued withdrawal of United States' military forces from Vietnam.

Peace. The signing of a peace treaty by North Vietnam, the Viet Cong, South Vietnam, and the United States occurred in Paris on January 17, 1973. The United States agreed to leave Vietnam within sixty days. Free elections to establish a new government were to be held in South Vietnam. After the United States withdrew, however, the North Vietnamese took over South Vietnam. In addition, Laos and Cambodia fell to the Communists in 1975.

Complete this activity.

5.18   The signing of a peace treaty by North Vietnam, the Viet Cong, South Vietnam, and the United

States occurred in _____ on January 17, 1973.

5.19   How many United States troops were in Vietnam by 1964? _____

KENNEDY TO CLINTON

Kennedy Administration. John Fitzgerald Kennedy was elected president in 1960. He was assassinated on November 22, 1963, after only two years and ten months in office. Kennedy won office on the basis of his New Frontier program to bring about changes that would be beneficial to the people of the United States. When Kennedy was elected, he faced domestic problems, such as racial tension, unemployment, and a slow economy. Kennedy appointed some of the ablest people in the country to help with the problems.

Civil rights demands were insistent. Black citizens wanted equal rights. To make their demands known they staged "freedom rides" to end segregation in public facilities and sit-ins in segregated restaurants.

To meet the demands, President Kennedy asked Congress for legislation to require public facilities be open to all citizens regardless of race. He also asked Congress to grant the attorney general, Robert Kennedy, authority to bring court cases to desegregate schools.

President Kennedy was assassinated before the bill was passed, but it passed during Lyndon Johnson's term of office. Kennedy's dealing with business affairs was direct. For example, when United States Steel Corporation raised the price of steel by $6 per ton in 1962, Kennedy denounced the action and the price increase was removed.

President Kennedy was sometimes accused of being anti-business, but he aided business by increasing benefits for companies investing in new equipment. In 1963, he proposed a tax cut applied to business as well as to the people.

Many of President Kennedy's New Frontier programs were bogged down in Congress. He was successful, however, in getting aid for economically depressed areas, a bill to increase federal minimum wage, and a Trade Expansion Act to lower tariffs.

Perhaps Kennedy's most remembered contribution occurred as a result of a Russian cosmonaut becoming the first human to orbit the earth. That event and the American spirit of competition allowed him to challenge the country to take the lead in the space race. Congress agreed to fund a program to put a man on the moon.

The Peace Corps was one of Kennedy's most popular programs. The plan sent Americans into underdeveloped countries as volunteers to teach the people ways of advancing their own countries economically.

In foreign affairs, President Kennedy faced the continued spread of communism and the threat of nuclear war. Secretary of Defense Robert McNamara favored a buildup of ground forces and less reliance on aircraft and missiles. McNamara believed that only with ground forces could the United States contain communism.

Kennedy's Alliance for Progress signaled a shift in attitudes of the United States toward Latin America. Although Latin America was not an aggressive threat, the poverty and discontent of the people was potentially dangerous. United States' investors in Latin America were associated with the ruling classes and the people often became anti-United States as a result. In addition, Communists used every opportunity to exploit unrest by promising distribution of wealth to the people. The Alliance for Progress was intended to provide funds for social programs and to help in promoting democratic institutions. Although the program was never fully realized, some improvements were made in education and in health care.

One of President Kennedy's most enduring programs was the Nuclear Test Ban Treaty that he signed with the Soviet Union in 1963. Russian nuclear tests in 1961 broke an unofficial test ban, which had endured for three years. After the Russians resumed their tests, the United States also began testing. At first the United States tests were underground, but later they resumed testing in the atmosphere over the Pacific Ocean. Both countries realized that they were endangering the health and the lives of people and agreed to sign the Nuclear Test Ban Treaty. Testing was still permitted underground, however.

Complete these statements.

5.20   The vocabulary word meaning *to affirm*, *to assert*, or *to declare* is _____ .

5.21   To be _____ is to be involved in some matter.

5.22   Kennedy's _____ was intended to provide funds for social
programs and to help in promoting democratic institutions.

Write the letter of the correct answer on the line.

5.23   How long had President Kennedy been in office when he was assassinated on November 22, 1963?

_____

    a. one year and ten months   b. two years and ten months
    c. two years and eleven months   d. three years

Johnson Administration. Recall that Lyndon Baines Johnson became president of the United States after John F. Kennedy was assassinated in Dallas. In 1964, Johnson was elected to a full term with 61 percent of the vote. Because Johnson had been a strong leader in Congress before he became vice president in the Kennedy Administration, the American people had confidence in him.

During his term in office, Johnson attempted to get through Congress legislation that Kennedy had proposed. He was only partially successful. He urged Congress to cut taxes for both individuals and corporations, and he announced that the federal budget would be less than the previous one. In addition, he also proposed the strong civil rights bill that Kennedy had supported, and it was signed into law in 1964. His own "War on Poverty" created new jobs and appropriated money that was to be spent in areas where the economy had faltered.

One of President Johnson's successes was delaying a railroad strike. The railroad owners and the union were in dispute over retaining firemen on trains even though the modern diesel locomotives no longer needed them. President Johnson arranged for a fifteen-day delay of the impending strike and ordered the company and union representatives to meet at the White House to work out a solution. Under that pressure the negotiating teams settled the disagreement in only twelve days.

President Johnson's program was known as the Great Society, and he was successful in getting many of his Great Society projects passed in Congress.

| The Civil Rights Act was passed during the Johnson Administration.

Among those projects was the Appalachia Bill to improve living standards in the Appalachian Mountain region. Proposals to increase federal aid to education, to cut excise taxes, and to provide stronger safety measures for automobiles were also passed.

President Johnson appointed the first black person to the cabinet and the first black man to the Supreme Court. Robert C. Weaver was secretary of housing and urban development and Thurgood Marshall was named a Supreme Court justice.

Health insurance for the aged known as Medicare was passed during President Johnson's administration. In addition, a voting rights bill was passed to ensure equality in voting for black people by forbidding literacy tests as a voting requirement.

As public pressure continued to build to end United States' involvement in Vietnam, President Johnson announced to the nation that he was stopping the bombing of North Vietnam to open the way for negotiations. He also surprised the nation by saying that he would neither seek nor accept the nomination for another term as president. Some people believe he sacrificed his political career for the cause of peace.

Complete these statements.

5.24 President Johnson's program to create new jobs and to appropriate money to faltering economic

areas was called War on _____ .

5.25 To end the _____ strike, President Johnson brought negotiators together at the White House until they worked out an agreement.

5.26 President Johnson's program to improve individual's rights and employment opportunities

was called the _____ .

5.27 President Johnson's health insurance plan for the elderly became known as

_____ .

5.28 To open the way for negotiations in Vietnam, President Johnson announced that he would

stop the a. _____ of b. _____ .

Nixon Administration. Republican Richard Nixon was elected president twice, in 1968 and in 1972. His election in 1968 was **predicated** upon the ending of the division over urban violence and campus riots that had occurred in the 1960s. The New Federalism was President Nixon's program of domestic reforms aimed at dismantling the Great Society program of Lyndon Johnson.

Under the New Federalism, Nixon proposed a minimum federal payment to every needy family with children. He also suggested revenue-sharing programs between the federal government and state and local governments. Congress approved revenue sharing, but balked at payments to needy families.

Although the Congress was Democratic and Nixon was a Republican, President Nixon was able to get some legislation passed. One of his proposals approved was the draft lottery. Congress also approved reforms in federal tax laws that increased personal income tax deductions and that cut tax benefits for foundations and oil companies. Congress also established the United States Postal Service to replace the Post Office Department that was reporting yearly deficits. In addition, Congress established Amtrak as an agency to operate passenger trains between the nation's cities. During President Nixon's term, Congress lowered the minimum voting age to eighteen for federal elections. That law became the Twenty-Sixth Amendment to the Constitution.

One of President Nixon's greatest problems was inflation. Prices were rising at a much higher rate than wage increases. President Nixon established a Pay Board to curb inflationary wage and salary increases and a Price Commission to regulate price increases. President Nixon ended most limits on wage and price increases, but prices continued to rise. By the end of 1971, inflation had risen to 8.8 percent nationally.

One of President Nixon's most controversial programs was his plan to build an antiballistic missile system called Safeguard. The plan, the president said, would protect United States bomber bases and ground missiles from enemy attack. Critics of the plan charged the system would step up the arms race and that the new missiles would cost too much. The plan was approved by a narrow margin in the Congress.

The Supreme Court made two major desegregation rulings during President Nixon's first administration. The Court in 1969 ruled that all public school districts must end segregation. The second ruling came in 1971 when the Court said that children should be bused to achieve integration in public schools in areas where state laws required segregation.

Also during Nixon's Administration, astronauts Neil A. Armstrong and Edwin E. Aldrin became the first people to set foot on the moon. Other space flights followed, but eventually NASA suffered severe budget cuts from Congress.

Environmental concerns drew attention during the Nixon Administration. People became concerned with pollution of the air, land, and water. In 1970, President Nixon established the Environmental Protection Agency to deal with pollution problems.

Nixon's greatest triumphs were undoubtedly in foreign relations. His Vietnam policy was labeled the Nixon Doctrine. The Nixon Doctrine did not propose abandonment of Asia altogether, but instead it proposed that Asian countries would take responsibility for their own defense.

When President Nixon began the bombing of Cambodia to drive out the Viet Cong, however, he received no support from Congress, who ordered a stop to the bombing. Another setback came when Congress overruled Nixon's veto of a resolution to limit presidential war powers.

An important political development occurred in Nixon's administration when the Soviet Union and the People's Republic of China began to disagree. They had long been rivals for world-Communist leadership. The split indicated that communism was not a unified ideology. Later, China invited President Nixon to visit that country. In February of 1972, Nixon and the Chinese leaders talked. Although the visit had little real importance at the time, it was symbolically significant.

The Watergate scandal was the downfall of Richard Nixon. In 1972, a burglary of Democratic Party headquarters in the Watergate complex in Washington, D.C. became headline news. Employees of President Nixon's reelection committee were arrested and convicted of burglary. Evidence uncovered later **implicated** top White House aides with either the break-in or the cover-up of the break-in. Nixon said that he had nothing to do with any of the occurrences. A Senate investigating committee learned that Nixon had secretly taped conversations in his office. When the courts ordered him to turn

| Nixon's Congress approved Amtrak as an agency to operate trains between American cities.

over the tapes, he offered summaries of them. In the meantime, Vice President Spiro Agnew resigned. Agnew was under investigation for accepting illegal payments while in office. President Nixon named Gerald R. Ford as Agnew's successor.

Impeachment hearings against President Nixon began in October, 1973, before the House Judiciary Committee. In July 1974, the committee finished reviewing evidence and voted to recommend three articles of impeachment against the president.

| The EPA has done much to control and eliminate pollution and waste in the environment.

Nixon was charged with obstructing justice by delaying the Watergate burglary investigation, attempting to hide the identities of people who ordered the burglary, abusing presidential powers, and disobeying subpoenas. On August 9, 1974, Nixon submitted his resignation as president; and Vice President Gerald R. Ford was sworn in as the thirty-eighth president of the United States. President Nixon's resignation ended the debates over his proposed impeachment, but many Americans continued to advocate prosecution for his role in the Watergate cover up. However, on September 8, President Ford pardoned Nixon of all federal crimes he may have committed while he was president.

Complete this activity.

5.29 List three ways in which Congress kept Richard Nixon's power in check during the years he was president.

_____

_____

_____

Put a check beside the correct answer(s).

5.30 Which of these demonstrate President Nixon's expertise in foreign relations matters?

_____ Nixon Doctrine

_____ Visit to China

_____ the New Federalism

_____ Safeguard program

5.31 Which three bills did President Nixon propose to Congress that aided United States' citizens?

_____ Trade Expansion Act

_____ Price Commission

_____ Appalachia Bill

_____ draft lottery

_____ Medicare

_____ Environmental Protection Agency

Ford Administration. Gerald Ford received his B.A. from the University of Michigan and a law degree from Yale. He served in the navy and in 1948 was elected to the House of Representatives for 14 terms. He replaced Spiro Agnew as vice president in 1973 and became president on August 9, 1974 when Nixon resigned and Nelson Rockefeller became vice president.

President Ford promptly pardoned President Nixon, an act which damaged Ford's early popularity. Shortly after he pardoned Richard Nixon, President Ford announced an amnesty program for draft dodgers and army deserters of the Vietnam War. To achieve amnesty, the men would have to work for two years in public service jobs. Of the estimated 106,000 eligible for amnesty, about 22,000 applied for amnesty under the program.

Inflation continued to be a problem. President Ford established, with congressional approval, the Council on Wage and Price Stability to uncover any inflationary wage and price increases. Ford also proposed tax increases for corporations and for citizens. The latter plans were dropped when the nation entered a recession. As inflation stabilized, unemployment soared. By May of 1975, the rate of unemployment reached 9 percent, the highest unemployment rate since 1941.

Ford's presidency was short and plagued by inflation. Ford vetoed 50 plus bills he thought inflationary. Congress passed few administration proposals. He argued in vain for help for South Vietnam as North Vietnam took over in 1975. In the 1976 presidential campaign, President Ford was challenged by former Governor James E. Carter. President Ford promised to continue the policies that brought economic recovery and that slowed the inflation rate. Carter charged Ford with mismanagement of the economy. Carter, a Democrat, defeated President Ford to become the next president of the United States.

Complete this activity.

5.32   List two ways that President Ford dealt with inflation and unemployment.

_____

_____

Complete these statements.

5.33   Ford's administration was plagued by the problem of _____ .

5.34   An unpopular move by Ford was the _____ of Nixon.

Carter Administration. James Earl Carter graduated from the Naval Academy in 1946, served in the navy and returned to Georgia to manage the family peanut business. State senator in 1962, governor in 1970, he ran for the presidency in 1976 on the Democratic ticket.

During his term he pardoned draft evaders and reviewed cases of deserters during the Vietnam War. He added the Departments of Energy and Education to his cabinet. He developed the cruise missile rather than the B-1 bomber and established a traditional energy program. Economic problems cut into his popularity.

His foreign policy was based on his Christian view of human rights. He used economic power against repressive governments and pushed the Soviets to allow Jews to migrate to Israel. In 1978, he brought Anwar Sadat of Egypt and Menachem Begin of Israel to Camp David to resolve their differences. The result of the hard negotiation was the Camp David Accord, a treaty between Egypt and Israel.

The Iran Hostage Crisis was one of his greatest problems. The Shah, an absolute sovereign, angered the citizens of Iran with his oppression and a revolution led by the Ayatollah Khomeini sent him into exile. They hated the United States for its support of the Shah. The United States allowed the Shah to enter the country for medical treatment. Iranian radicals took the staff of the United States Embassy hostage and the government refused to do anything. Carter refused to meet the terrorists' demands, suspended relations with Iran, and froze its assets in the United States. A disastrous rescue attempt in April of 1980 failed and the hostages were held for 444 days until the Reagan Administration. Double-digit inflation and the Iran Crisis contributed to his defeat in 1980 by Ronald Reagan.

Answer *true* **or** *false*.

5.35 _____ Carter was a native of Georgia.

5.36 _____ Inflation was not a problem of the Carter Administration.

5.37 _____ Carter based his foreign policy on Christian principles.

5.38 _____ Carter had the Iranian hostages freed.

5.39 _____ Carter negotiated peace between Egypt and Israel.

Reagan Administration. Ronald Reagan was born in Illinois and earned a degree from Eureka College. In California he became an actor, served as president of the Screen Actors Guild and served two terms as governor of California. He ran for president and was elected in 1980. A conservative in foreign policy, he instituted anti-communist policies abroad. Reagan favored less government, but his economic policies were not so conservative.

His economic plan, named Reaganomics, called for tax cuts—reductions in Federal spending—with the exception of a huge military budget. Although there was an income tax cut in 1981, there was also the largest tax increase ever in 1982. In his eight years, the deficit grew from $30+ billion to about $1.6–$2.0 trillion.

He solved the air traffic controllers' strike in 1981, appointed the first woman Supreme Court justice, Sandra Day O'Connor, and initiated the Star Wars Defense System. He was injured by a would-be assassin in 1981.

His tenure was tainted by the Iran-Contra scandal wherein his staff sold weapons to Iran in the hope that the American hostages would be released. The profits were used, against the direct order of Congress, to help the Contras fighting the communist government of Nicaragua. Hostages were released, but later convictions were over turned and President Bush pardoned the rest. The deficit still was the hottest issue.

Match the following.

5.40 _____ Sandra Day O'Connor

5.41 _____ Iran-Contra

5.42 _____ Star Wars

5.43 _____ conservative

5.44 _____ Reaganomics

5.45 _____ 444 days

a. scandalous crime deal with Iran

b. Ronald Reagan

c. length of hostage captivity

d. first woman Supreme Court justice

e. missile defense system

f. Reagan's economic plan

George H. W. Bush Administration. George H. W. Bush was a navy pilot during World War II. He received a degree in economics from Yale in 1948. He started at the bottom in the oil business in Texas and earned a fortune. He was elected a representative in the Texas legislature in 1966 and 1968; chairman of the Republican Party in 1972; United States envoy to China in 1974; Director of CIA in 1975; vice president under Reagan 1980–1988.

Bush was elected president in 1988. He was a moderate and did not match Reagan's popularity. He had to face the Savings and Loan crisis and the subsequent bailout of the industry for $400 billion dollars, so he raised taxes although he had promised not to. His conduct of the Persian Gulf War (Desert Storm) against Iraq was exemplary.

Clinton Administration. Bill Clinton received a degree from Georgetown in 1968 and a law degree from Yale in 1973. He was attorney general of Arkansas in 1977 and a governor for ten years beginning in 1978. He was elected president in 1992. He and his wife led a task force to reform health care and developed a plan for universal coverage. It was defeated by a Democratic Congress.

He lifted abortion restrictions and appointed a second woman to the Supreme Court. His legislative agenda included laws that required companies to grant unpaid leaves for family needs and a ban on assault weapons. He suffered a political setback in congressional elections of 1994. The Republicans won control of both houses and they engaged in a battle over budgets and reduction of deficit. This caused the shut down of the government in 1995 during negotiations. Clinton was the second president impeached in 1998 when he lied under oath in a lawsuit. He was not removed from office at his trial in 1999.

Answer *true* **or** *false*.

5.46	_____	The Persian Gulf War was against Iran.
5.47	_____	George H. W. Bush hailed from Georgia.
5.48	_____	George H. W. Bush's political philosophy was moderate.
5.49	_____	George H. W. Bush directed the CIA.
5.50	_____	George H. W. Bush raised taxes.
5.51	_____	Clinton ran on the Republican ticket.
5.52	_____	Clinton was impeached for lying under oath.
5.53	_____	Clinton's agenda included unpaid leaves from companies for family needs.

GEORGE W. BUSH TO TRUMP

George W. Bush Administration. George W. Bush graduated from Yale in 1968 and Harvard Business School in 1975. He served as the governor of Texas for six years before becoming President of the U.S. He was the Republican party's nominee and elected president in 2000 and 2004 serving for eight years. His presidency was largely defined by the September 11, 2001, terrorist attacks and their aftermath.

The terrorist attacks caught the U.S. by surprise. In their wake, the George W. Bush administration established the office of Homeland Security. This office was charged with protecting the United States and its borders from terrorist threats. The U.S. also sent soldiers to Afghanistan to dismantle the government that had supported terrorists as well as to find terrorist leaders. The U.S. military also went to war in Iraq to root out threats from that nation.

At home, George W. Bush worked with Congress to pass the "No Child Left Behind" legislation. This legislation raised educational standards. Schools were accountable for their students' progress, and penalties were put in place for schools whose students were not succeeding. George W. Bush's term ended with a global economic crisis that threatened nations around the world.

Obama Administration. Barack Obama graduated from Columbia University in 1983 and Harvard Law School in 1991. He was elected a U.S. Senator from Illinois in 2004 and served for four years. In 2008 Obama was the Democratic nominee for President and was elected that fall. He took office in January of 2009 as the first African-American President of the United States.

The Obama administration came into office in the midst of a global economic crisis. The nation was also at war in both Iraq and Afghanistan. During his first term in office he appointed two justices to the Supreme Court. The first was Sonia Sotomayor, the first Hispanic American Supreme Court Justice, and the second was Elena Kagan. On May 1, 2011, President Obama announced that the leader of Al-Qaeda, Osama Bin Laden, who claimed responsibility for the terrorist attacks on September 11, 2001, had been killed. Also during President Obama's first term, the Patient Protection and Affordable Care Act became law which added significant regulations to the U. S. healthcare system. The withdrawal of all U. S. troops from Iraq was completed in December of 2011.

In 2012, Obama was elected to a second term. The president's focus during this term tended to be on social and climate issues. Unfortunately, due to the rise of the Islamic State of Iraq and the Levant (ISIL), troops were sent back to Iraq in 2014.

Donald J. Trump Administration. Donald Trump graduated from the Wharton School of the University of Pennsylvania in 1968 with a degree in economics. He became a highly successful real estate developer with properties in New York City, in other major U.S. cities, and in some international locations. Becoming the Republican nominee over a field of 17 other major challengers, he won the 2016 presidential race over the first female candidate, Hillary Clinton. Trump was the fifth president in history to take office despite losing the popular vote but by winning the Electoral College vote. During his first 100 days in office, Trump signed 24 executive orders, the most of any president since World War II.

| Donald J. Trump

Answer *true* **or** *false.*

5.54 _____ George W. Bush was governor of California before being elected president.

5.55 _____ The "No Child Left Behind" legislation was designed to improve schools.

5.56 _____ The Office of Homeland Security was responsible for protecting the president.

5.57 _____ A global economic crisis threatened the U.S. and other nations at the beginning of George W. Bush's presidency.

5.58 _____ Barack Obama was the first African American president.

5.59 _____ Donald Trump won the popular vote in the 2016 presidential election.

5.60 _____ Obama graduated from Harvard Business School.

5.61 _____ Obama served as a U.S. Senator from Illinois before being elected president.

↻ **Review the material in this section in preparation for the Self Test.** The Self Test will check your mastery of this particular section as well as your knowledge of the previous sections.

SELF TEST 5

Answer *true* **or** *false* (each answer, 1 point).

5.01 _____ The effects of depression in Europe were partly responsible for World War II.

5.02 _____ Paul von Hindenburg appointed Adolf Hitler president of Germany.

5.03 _____ Italy, Germany, and the United States were members of the Axis Powers in World War II.

5.04 _____ The United States declared war on Japan because of the bombing of Pearl Harbor.

5.05 _____ The United Nations was established at the end of World War II.

5.06 _____ President Kennedy offered to send military advisors to Korea during the Korean conflict.

5.07 _____ President Johnson ordered the bombing of a North Vietnamese port after several United States advisors were killed.

5.08 _____ One of the terms of the Vietnam treaty was the provision for free elections in South Vietnam.

5.09 _____ President Nixon was found guilty of the impeachment charges.

5.010 _____ President Johnson was the originator of the civil rights legislation that was eventually passed by Congress.

5.011 _____ Carter based his foreign policy on Christian human rights.

Match the following (each answer, 2 points).

5.012	_____ Eli Whitney	**a.**	president during the Civil War
5.013	_____ Woodrow Wilson	**b.**	assembly line production
5.014	_____ Henry Ford	**c.**	invented the airplane
5.015	_____ Thomas Jefferson	**d.**	the League of Nations
5.016	_____ Alexander Hamilton	**e.**	invented the printing press
5.017	_____ William Penn	**f.**	standardized parts
5.018	_____ Jefferson Davis	**g.**	president of Confederacy
5.019	_____ Abraham Lincoln	**h.**	wrote the Declaration of Independence
5.020	_____ Wilbur and Orville Wright	**i.**	wrote financial plan for the United States
5.021	_____ Johann Gutenberg	**j.**	founded Pennsylvania

Write the letter of the correct answer on each line (each answer, 2 points).

5.022   The event that led to the United States' involvement in World War I was _____ .

a. the assassination of Austrian Archduke Ferdinand
b. Britain's declaration of war
c. the bombing of the *Maine*
d. Germany's sinking of United States supply ships

5.023   Kennedy won the presidency on the basis of his program for _____ .

a. civil rights   b. getting the United States out of Vietnam
c. dealing with inflation   d. a New Frontier

5.024   Kennedy's program that signaled a shift in attitude of the United States toward Latin America was

called the _____ .

a. Test Ban Treaty   b. New Frontier   c. Alliance for Progress   d. Great Society

5.025   Lyndon Johnson helped settle a potential railroad strike by _____ .

a. ordering men back to work   b. holding negotiations at the White House
c. calling in federal troops   d. talking with union leaders

5.026   Richard Nixon's plan for dismantling the Great Society programs was called _____ .

a. the Nixon Doctrine   b. the New Deal   c. the New Federalism   d. the Pay Board

5.027   During Richard Nixon's administration, the Supreme Court made two major desegregation rulings.

One of them stated that _____ .

a. all public school districts must end segregation
b. all poll taxes must be abolished
c. black people may have equal access to public facilities
d. black people must have equal access to housing

5.028   Because of the concerns of the public about pollution, Richard Nixon established _____ .

a. the Nixon Doctrine   b. the Federal Trade Commission
c. the Environmental Protection Agency   d. the New Federalism

5.029   The _____ defined the George W. Bush presidency.

a. war in Iraq
b. September 11, 2001 terrorist attacks
c. global economic crisis

5.030   Barack Obama was the first _____ elected President of the United States.

a. U.S. Senator   b. single man   c. African-American

Complete these statements (each answer, 3 points).

5.031   List two causes of World War II.

_____

_____

5.032   The United States became involved in World War II because of the attack on

_____ .

5.033   Members of the Axis Powers were _____ , _____ ,

and _____ .

5.034   Members of the Allied Powers were the_____ , _____ ,

and the _____ .

5.035   The first step in President Nixon's program of Vietnamization was the _____
of service men.

5.036   The hostages were held by Iran during the presidency of _____ .

5.037   President Nixon _____ because Congress was going to impeach him.

Match the following (each answer, 2 points).

5.038   _____   Richard Nixon

5.039   _____   Gerald Ford

5.040   _____   John F. Kennedy

5.041   _____   James E. Carter

5.042   _____   Robert McNamara

5.043   _____   Adolph Hitler

5.044   _____   Lieutenant Colonel James
Doolittle

5.045   _____   Dwight D. Eisenhower

5.046   _____   Harry S. Truman

5.047   _____   Douglas MacArthur

5.048   _____   Syngman Rhee

5.049   _____   Lyndon Johnson

5.050   _____   Sir Walter Raleigh

5.051   _____   Franklin D. Roosevelt

5.052   _____   James Monroe

a. pardoned Richard Nixon

b. New Deal

c. Watergate

d. said that Europe should stay out of the affairs
of American countries

e. New Frontier

f. organized the Roanoke Island Colony

g. defeated Gerald Ford in 1976

h. Great Society

i. Defense Department under President
Kennedy

j. head of South Korean government

k. Nazi dictator

l. commander of United States' ground forces in
Korea

m. led bomb attack on Tokyo

n. president of the United States during the
Korean War

o. commander of United States troops in Europe
in World War II

Match the following (each answer, 2 points).

5.053	_____	amnesty
5.054	_____	Carter
5.055	_____	cruise missile
5.056	_____	Menachem Begin
5.057	_____	Anwar Sadat
5.058	_____	George H. W. Bush
5.059	_____	$400 billion
5.060	_____	Budget debate
5.061	_____	first shuttle
5.062	_____	environment
5.063	_____	abortion
5.064	_____	Great Depression
5.065	_____	Hiroshima
5.066	_____	Korea
5.067	_____	Iraq

a. Government shutdown 1995
b. invaded Kuwait
c. forgive desertion, etc.
d. Chinese "volunteers" helped the North
e. peanut farmer
f. atomic bomb
g. preferred over the B-1 bomber
h. stock market crash
i. treaty with Egypt
j. divisive issue
k. president of Egypt
l. control of pollution
m. head of CIA
n. Columbia
o. Savings and Loan bailout

6. CLOSING OUT THE TWENTIETH CENTURY

Section Objectives

Review this objective. When you have completed this section, you should be able to:

22. Explain international events that have occurred in recent years.

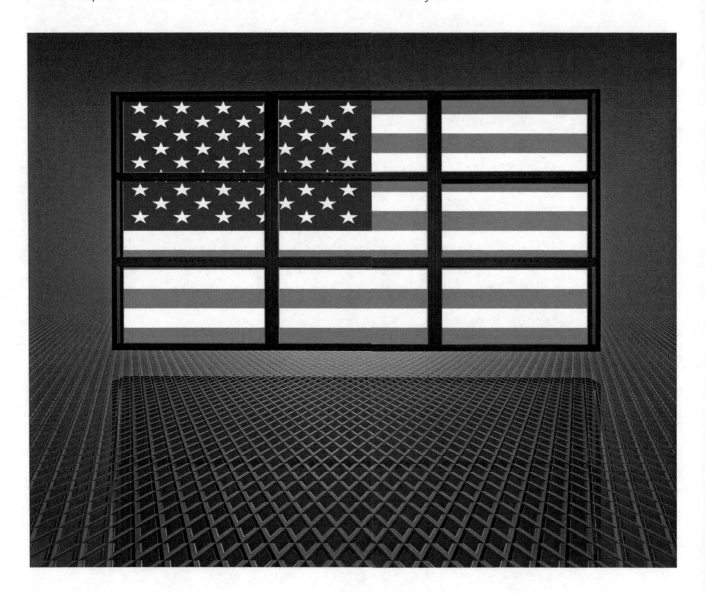

THE UNITED STATES

The Shuttle Program. It began when *Columbia*, the first reusable spacecraft, flew on April 12, 1981. The program made earth orbit possible for various space projects and also made passenger travel possible for people from various walks of life. As of 2000, there had been about 100 American space shuttle flights.

The greatest scientific and technological achievements of the shuttle program include: putting satellites into orbit, servicing spacecraft in orbit, and the launching of the Hubble telescope together with its repair. The program suffered a great tragedy when on January 28, 1986, the shuttle, *Challenger*, blew up killing the crew including a school teacher, Christa

McAuliffe. Then, on February 1st, 2003, tragedy struck again as the *Columbia* blew up while reentering the earth's atmosphere. America mourned the loss of all seven courageous astronauts. The final shuttle mission took place in July of 2011.

The Deficit. The largest economic issues were the federal deficit and the national debt. The United States had no balanced budget between 1969 and 1999. In 1992, the deficit was $290 billion dollars, the national debt was $4.351 trillion dollars, and the government paid $296 billion in interest.

The deficit was a constant issue that politicians promised to correct by cutting government programs, but nothing was accomplished until 1998. A proposal for a constitutional amendment to balance the budget by the year 2000 failed to pass in Congress. However, increased revenues improved the situation at the end of the 1990s.

The Environment. Much attention has been given in the 1980s and 1990s to environmental issues involving natural resources and the atmosphere. The preservation of natural beauty includes the care of endangered species as well as the maintenance of lands and parks. It also includes the purification of the air, land, and watersheds.

Abortion. Abortion became a moral and a political issue during the '90s. Abortion was legalized by the Supreme Court in 1973. Supporters argue that the mother has the right of control over her body and that the fetus is only tissue; therefore, no moral obligations are to be attached. The opponents argue that the fetus is a child and as such has the rights belonging to human life.

The opposition to abortion came primarily from Christian groups such as Right to Life. The issue of abortion gave unity to Christian political and social activity in politics. Some groups demonstrated at abortion clinics and at the homes of practitioners. The pro-abortion forces reacted sharply and looked to the courts and laws for relief.

Christian Political Activism. Christians have a long history of activism in the United States dealing in the past with such issues as slavery and alcohol. More recent issues have included abortion, prayer in schools, homosexuality, educational concerns, and irresponsible government.

The Moral Majority was an attempt in 1979 to organize Christian voters. It disbanded after moral scandals adversely affected the leadership of several prominent television evangelists. In the 1990s these goals were picked up by the Christian Coalition. It concentrated on grass roots organization to influence government at the lower level. An example of Christian grassroots attack on political problems is the moral approach of Promise Keepers, a men's group dedicated to Christ, the family, and good relations with others.

Trade. The '90s saw a trade deficit of $150 billion dollars. Congress has had to deal with countries which have unfair trade practices. Most countries of the European community have been interested in free trade with the United States. However, Japan, which has unfairly restricted American trade, has created a $65 billion trade deficit alone. China has also violated fair trade laws by its infringement of copyright and patent laws on its imports.

The United States has attempted free trade with its neighbors through the North American Free Trade Agreement with Canada and Mexico. NAFTA took effect on January 1, 1994. Its conditions not only dealt with trade items but with the environment as well. The pros and cons of the agreement are still being argued and the verdict is still out.

Education. In 2001, President George W. Bush and Congress worked together to pass the No Child Left Behind legislation. School districts were given additional funds as long as students met set academic standards. States and school districts received greater flexibility and support from the government as long as student performance goals were met. However, schools were penalized if they could not demonstrate that students were progressing. Schools would now receive report cards just like those given to students. After years of criticism from both the right and the left, a bill was introduced to Congress on April 30, 2015, to replace the No Child Left Behind Act, the Every Student Succeeds Act, which was passed by the House on December 2 and the Senate on December 9, before being signed into law by President Obama on December 10, 2015. This bill affords states more flexibility in regards to setting their own respective standards for measuring school as well as student performance.

The Nation. Natural disasters have been in the headlines frequently in the New Millennium. Hurricane Katrina devastated the city of New Orleans in 2005. Much of the city was flooded and people were forced from their homes. Once the water receded the amount of destruction done to the city became apparent. The city of New Orleans continues the process of rebuilding and finding ways of protecting their city from hurricane threats.

Another issue affecting the U.S. is illegal immigration. Immigrants from Mexico and Central America illegally cross the United States' southern border. Seeking better lives, these immigrants find jobs where they can work illegally in the U.S. The government, businesses, and others need to work together to find suitable solutions to the problem of illegal immigration.

School shootings are another problem facing the U.S. Shootings at Columbine High School in 1999 shocked the nation. Thirteen people were killed by two classmates bent on destruction. School shootings took place in other cities and towns in the U.S. with devastating effects. The worst school shooting took place at Virginia Tech in 2007 where 32 people were killed by one gunman. School shootings have been becoming more frequent since the concern began. Between Columbine and the end of the 2018 school year, there were 68 school shootings. Law enforcement officials, teachers, parents, and others have worked together to find ways to end school violence.

Terrorism Strikes Home. The modern phenomenon of terrorism, which much of the world has experienced repeatedly, rocked the United States in a remarkable way on September 11, 2001. On that infamous day, hijacked commercial airlines were flown into the twin towers of the World Trade Center in New York, causing those majestic skyscrapers to fall to the streets below, resulting in unthinkable devastation and loss of life. Another airliner smashed into the side of the Pentagon, causing enormous destruction and death. The hijack of a third aircraft—presumably headed for the Capitol—was thwarted, causing the plane to crash to the ground in Pennsylvania. By the end of the day, thousands of Americans were killed in the attacks or in attempts to rescue victims.

The social and political fallout from that dreadful day has profoundly affected the way we think, the way we live, and what we believe. We are challenged not only to be aware of what happened and how it happened, but also how to think about and interpret why it happened.

Responding to the attack on America, President George W. Bush declared a "war on terrorism." The former Pennsylvania governor Tom Ridge was appointed as the first head of the new Office of Homeland Security, and later became secretary of the newly formed Department of Homeland Security. Security measures were intensified at significant locations and events around the country. Military troops from around the world joined U.S. forces in an invasion of Afghanistan, seeking to root out terrorist leaders and destroy terrorist organizations, particularly Osama bin Laden and the Taliban-sponsored al Qaeda international terrorist network.

INTERNATIONAL SCENE

Lebanon. Lebanon in the Middle East is a country divided by civil war. Muslims aided by the PLO (Palestine Liberation Organization) used bases in Lebanon to attack Israel. In 1982, Israel invaded Lebanon to get rid of the PLO. The PLO agreed to leave and UN (United Nations) forces ensured safe departure. Lebanon asked UN forces to maintain peace after the assassination of the president-elect of Lebanon and a massacre in a refugee camp threatened civil war.

President Reagan sent Marines as part of the peacekeeping force, but in 1983 a suicidal terrorist drove a van of explosives into the marine barracks, killing 241 soldiers. Another attack killed an additional 54 soldiers. Terrorist activities such as kidnapping hostages, hijacking jets, brutal beatings, and murder have continued. The United States has taken a hard line with terrorists and has refused to negotiate with them.

Grenada. This Caribbean island with a population of about 8,000 was the victim of a Communist coup in 1983. The United States invaded Grenada in order to restore safety and order to the island. U.S. forces departed before the end of the year.

Terrorism. Terrorism occurs when a group of people united in a common cause attack innocent people in an attempt to further their objective. While numerous groups have used terrorist methods to achieve their goals, at the beginning of the 21st century, an international terrorist network called al Qaeda adopted these methods resulting in death and destruction in many parts of the world.

In October of 2000, the *USS Cole* was attacked while in port in Yemen. Seventeen U.S. sailors were killed by terrorists. As a result of the 9/11 attack against the

World Trade Center and the Pentagon, the United States and its allies went to war in Afghanistan and Iraq in an effort to stop the terrorism efforts of al-Qaeda and other militant Muslim groups.

The terrorist attacks of al-Qaeda were not only against the United States. Terrorists targeted a night club in Bali, Indonesia, filled with Australian tourists in 2002. Over 200 Australians were killed in the attack. Ten bombs on four trains in Spain exploded in March of 2004, killing over 150 people and injuring 1,500. In July of 2005, bombs destroyed three trains and buses in London and killed 52 people. Terrorists continue to carry out attacks against innocent people. Many of these al Qaeda attacks occur in largely Muslim countries where people are seeking peace.

Panama. Manuel Noriega, the dictator who ran Panama in the '80s, was indicted by the United States for operating a drug-smuggling ring. The president of Panama tried to fire Noriega but Noriega took over without elections. In December of 1989 the United States invaded the Canal Zone to protect the Americans in the zone, arrested Noriega, and sent him to the United States for trial.

The Cold War. The standoff between the United States and the Soviet Union had gone on since the end of World War II. In 1985, Mikhail Gorbachev assumed power and began to change the Soviet Union. He called his reforms "glasnost" (openness) and "perestroika" (restructuring). Ideas and information were opened up for discussion between the two world powers. He subsequently initiated capitalistic reforms into the Soviet economic system, removed troops from Afghanistan, and pursued agreements over arms and trade.

President Reagan didn't trust Gorbachev because of the long history of deceit by the U.S.S.R. However, President George H. W. Bush did meet with Gorbachev. The two of them agreed to destroy most of their countries' chemical, nuclear, and conventional weapons.

The Communist Party in satellite nations was deactivated. Hungary initiated measures for freedom in 1989 and finally dissolved the Communist Party. The Berlin Wall was taken down in 1989. In 1990, East and West Germany were reunited. In 1991, greater autonomy was given to former republics. A hard line Communist coup was attempted in Russia.

However, President Boris Yeltsin, the president of Russia, called for demonstrations against the coup and it consequently failed. Soviet republics declared themselves independent and on December 26, 1991, the Union of Soviet Socialist Republics dissolved.

Persian Gulf War. On August 2, 1990, Iraq invaded and annexed Kuwait. The United States with UN support formed a coalition to remove the Iraqis. With a force involving 39 nations, the coalition began on January 17, 1991 to drive the Iraqi military out of Kuwait. On February 24, 1991 UN forces then invaded Iraq. The fighting lasted only 100 hours.

Iraq accepted the terms of the cease-fire and promised to destroy weapons stockpiles and pay damages to Kuwait. However, because Saddam Hussein refused to properly comply, an economic embargo was placed on Iraq. Hussein ordered Kuwaiti oil wells to be set on fire.

The United States military and its allies invaded Iraq again in 2004. Iraq was suspected of harboring terrorists as well as weapons. Saddam Hussein continued to terrorize his own people. Hussein was removed from office and fled to the countryside. Eventually he was found, tried, and condemned for murdering his own subjects. The United States worked with the Iraqi people to set up a new democratic government.

Israel and the PLO. The success of the Persian Gulf War added tremendously to American prestige and standing in the world, particularly in the Middle East. Shortly after the war, the first serious negotiations developed between the Palestinians and Israel over the creation of a homeland for Palestinian Arabs. Also, hostages held in Lebanon were released. The more moderate Arab nations such as Kuwait became firmer American allies.

Bosnia. During the Cold War, Bosnia was part of communist Yugoslavia. It has a population of Serbs, Croats, and Muslims with a long history of violence among them. When Communist rule ended, civil war immediately broke out and the Serbs grabbed two-thirds of the country. Muslims and Croats reached a cease-fire in 1994, but Yugoslavian support for Bosnian Serbs brought embargoes and condemnation from the West. Truce talks in 1995 resulted in an agreement to divide the nation. In 1998, Bosnia was again on the verge of civil war. Further violence occurred in the Serbian province of Kosovo in 1999.

Afghanistan. The home base for the terrorists of 9/11 was Afghanistan. Osama bin Laden, who masterminded the attack, operated terrorist camps in the country. Following the attack against the United States, bin Laden and those closest to him are thought to have fled to the mountainous regions of the country. The Taliban, who ruled Afghanistan, harbored bin Laden and his al Qaeda terrorist organization. The U. S. and its allies invaded Afghanistan in an attempt to capture bin Laden and remove the Taliban from power. The Taliban government was soon replaced by a democratically elected government.

Complete these statements.

6.1 The name of the school teacher who died on the shuttle *Challenger* was

_____ .

6.2 The most famous piece of equipment launched from a shuttle in earth's orbit was the

_____ .

6.3 Before the U.S. and its allies invaded, the government of _____
was run by the Taliban.

6.4 The Caribbean island that the United States invaded in 1983 was _____ .

6.5 The No Child Left Behind legislation was promoted by President _____ .

6.6 _____ caused extensive damage to the city of New
Orleans in 2005.

6.7 The dictator of Panama that the United States removed was _____ .

Answer *true* **or** *false*.

6.8 _____ Osama bin Laden had terrorist camps in the nation of Afghanistan.

6.9 _____ The school shooting at Columbine High School left 3 students dead.

6.10 _____ In 2005, terrorists bombed the London subway.

6.11 _____ Most illegal immigrants enter the United States through its northwestern border.

Write the letter of the correct answer on each line.

6.12 The United States is most concerned about _____ .

a. Russian and the Ukraine in matters of trade
c. Malaysia and Indonesia in matters of trade
b. Mexico and Canada in matters of trade
d. Japan and China in matters of trade

6.13 The United States has a trade agreement with Canada and Mexico called _____ .

a. the American Trade Contract
c. the North American Free Trade Agreement
b. the America's Trade Unit
d. the North-South Amity

6.14 The name of the 1983 report on education which showed that the United States was at the bottom

in comparison to industrialized nations is _____ .

a. The Senate Report on Education
b. Education for the '90s
c. A Nation at Risk
d. SAT and Illiteracy

6.15 The Soviet leader who changed the Soviet world was _____ .

a. Boris Yeltsin
b. Mikhail Gorbachev
c. Leonid Brezhnev
d. Alexi Andropov

6.16 The republics of the U.S.S.R. declared themselves _____ .

a. satellites
b. counties
c. independent countries
d. a federation

6.17 The most bitter representation of communism in East Germany was _____ .

a. the chancellery
b. the bandstag
c. the Berlin Gate
d. the Berlin Wall

6.18 East and West Germans were united in _____ .

a. 1990
b. 1991
c. 1992
d. 1993

6.19 In 1990, Iraq invaded the nation of _____ .

a. Iran
b. Yemen
c. Bahrain
d. Kuwait

6.20 The land war with Iraq in the Persian Gulf War lasted _____ .

a. six days
b. 100 hours
c. one week

6.21 Bosnia was formerly a part of _____ .

a. Yugoslavia
b. Sarajevo
c. Croatia
d. Serbia

6.22 Peace ended in Bosnia when _____ .

a. foreign aid ended
b. communism ended
c. when the name changed

Before you take this last Self Test, you may want to do one or more of these self checks.

1. _____ Read the objectives. Determine if you can do them.
2. _____ Restudy the material related to any objectives that you cannot do.
3. _____ Use the **SQ3R** study procedure to review the material:
   a. **S**can the sections.
   b. **Q**uestion yourself again (review the questions you wrote initially).
   c. **R**ead to answer your questions.
   d. **R**ecite the answers to yourself.
   e. **R**eview areas you did not understand.
4. _____ Review all vocabulary, activities, and Self Tests, writing a correct answer for every wrong answer.

SELF TEST 6

Complete these statements (each answer, 3 points).

6.01   The space shuttle program began on April 12, _____ .

6.02   The name of that first shuttle was _____ .

6.03   One of the great technological feats of the shuttle program was putting the

_____ telescope into orbit and going back to repair it.

6.04   A tragedy of the shuttle program came when a. _____ ,

a school teacher, died in the explosion of the b. _____ .

6.05   The president forced to resign by the Watergate Scandal was _____ .

6.06   Osama bin Laden led a terrorists group called _____ .

6.07   The majority of illegal immigrants cross at the _____ border of the
United States.

Write the letter of the correct answer on each line (each answer, 3 points).

6.08   The worst school shooting took place at _____ .

a. Columbine High School   b. Rosewood Middle School
c. University of Maryland   d. Virginia Tech

6.09   Terrorists bombed the _____ in London, England in 2005.

a. airport   b. subway   c. train station   d. Tower of London

6.010   The group in charge of Afghanistan when the U.S. and its allies invaded was called _____ .

a. al Qaeda   b. the Marshalls   c. the Taliban   d. the Righteous

6.011   The trade deficit in the United States is usually blamed on _____ .

a. Iraq   b. Iran   c. Kuwait   d. Japan and China

6.012   The United States has a free trade agreement with _____ .

a. the common market   b. Malaysia and Borneo
c. Mexico and Canada   d. Uruguay and Paraguay

6.013   The legislation passed by Congress and supported by President George W. Bush was called _____ .

a. Save our Schools   b. No Child Left Behind
c. The Iowa Tests of Basic Skills   d. Schools 101

6.014   The U.S. and its allies removed _____ from power in Iraq in 2004.

a. Hitler   b. Hussein   c. bin Laden   d. Baghdad

Match the following (each answer, 3 points).

6.015	_____	riot
6.016	_____	Great Flood of 1993
6.017	_____	train station
6.018	_____	Central America
6.019	_____	terrorist activities
6.020	_____	Grenada
6.021	_____	World Trade Center and Oklahoma City Federal Building
6.022	_____	Manuel Noriega
6.023	_____	Cold War

a. an island in the Caribbean invaded by the United States

b. Los Angeles

c. terrorist bombings in the United States

d. Mississippi River

e. Panamanian dictator

f. place from where many illegal immigrants to the United States come

g. United States and Soviet Union

h. place where the Madrid terrorist bombing took place

i. hijacking jets, kidnapping

Answer *true* **or** *false* (each answer, 3 points).

6.024	_____	The leader of Iraq in the Gulf War was Khomeini.
6.025	_____	The ally of the United States in the Gulf War was Kuwait.
6.026	_____	As a result of the Persian Gulf War, Iraq was placed under UN sanctions.
6.027	_____	Bosnia is part of the Ukraine.
6.028	_____	The conflict in Bosnia is among ethnic groups within the country.
6.029	_____	The war with Iraq lasted 100 hours.
6.030	_____	The leader of the Soviet Union when it dissolved was Mikhail Gorbachev.
6.031	_____	The reforms of Gorbachev were *glasnost* and *perestroika*.
6.032	_____	The Berlin Wall was an imaginary line in East Germany.
6.033	_____	Boris Yeltsin was the president of Russia when the U.S.S.R. split apart.

$\frac{82}{102}$ **SCORE** _____   ✓ **CHECK** _____ _____
Teacher   Date

Before taking the LIFEPAC Test, you may want to do one or more of these self checks.

1. _____ Read the objectives. Determine if you can do them.
2. _____ Restudy the material related to any objectives that you cannot do.
3. _____ Use the **SQ3R** study procedure to review the material.
4. _____ Review activities, Self Tests, and LIFEPAC vocabulary words.
5. _____ Restudy areas of weakness indicated by the last Self Test.